Questions Answered

Dear Jim,
Your fellow servant,

Larryn Young
01.16.2012

Questions Answered

Addressing Christian Theology

Larry N. Young

Library of Congress Control Number:		2011912214
ISBN:	Hardcover	978-1-4653-3698-9
	Softcover	978-1-4653-3697-2
	Ebook	978-1-4653-3699-6

This book was printed in the United States of America.

To order additional copies of this book, contact:
Xlibris Corporation
1-888-795-4274
www.Xlibris.com
Orders@Xlibris.com
102628

CONTENTS

Chapter 1

~ Does God Exist? ~

I remember a few years back reading about a wealthy individual who offered something like $25,000 to anyone who could prove to him that God existed. I supposed he was interested about the existence of God, because, if God did exist, then he would be concerned about what God might require of him. At the time, I considered what it would take to adequately prove to someone that God did exist. Then, I wondered why the individual was questioning the existence of God in the first place and why he did not already believe that God existed.

I began by considering a human being at birth. Are we born with anything that would cause us to believe or not to believe in the existence of a Creator God? As for facts or knowledge, it seemed to me that we start out with a blank slate. From there things could become very complicated. What we proceeded to learn would depend upon our parents, friends, teachers, et cetera. If our parents were atheists, we would probably be told to think that there is no God. If my friends and teachers also confirmed that, I could very well accept the premise that God did not exist.

Every conclusion in adult thinking begins with an initial premise. If the premise is correct, then my thinking will be correct. For example, if I have a premise that all flowers are red, and I say that this is a flower, my conclusion must be that it is red. But we know all flowers are not red, so my premise must be wrong. However, my premise may be difficult to evaluate.

My premise may be that there are no absolutes, except one, and that would be 'there are no absolutes'. If my thinking is then based upon the premise that there are no absolutes but you tell me that there are absolutes, then I must either reject your statement or you must show me that my premise is wrong.

Sometimes we must ask people why they have the premise that they have. It may be that it is just what they were told without any proof that it is, in fact, true. If I accepted as true every political promise that I heard and then used them as a premise for my thinking, you can only imagine how foolish my conclusions would be. The question really becomes how and why I selected the premise that I use to arrive at my conclusions.

For example, if my upbringing led me to the premise that 'there is no God', then my conclusion will be that there '*is not any God who is holding me accountable to any standard.*' If there is no God, then *there is not any one standard* exceeding *all other standards of right and wrong or at least what I want to choose as sociably acceptable conduct.* Additionally, if there is no God, then *only the standards set by me or by others who, by force, can affect me will have any meaning for me.* If it is only other people that I must be concerned with and if I can control them, then I can do pretty much as I please. If I am so inclined, the struggle for power will begin. If I am not so inclined, I will do whatever I think I can get away with, without causing others to get after me. Life then becomes what I can make it. Natural disasters, sickness, disease, accidents and behavior of others, et cetera, are just things I will have to contend with until I die and then there is nothing—just as it was before I was born.

This attitude may represent the practical lives of many people in our community, along with a lot of politicians and, certainly, the world at large. Many religious people are, in actuality, practicing atheists. They are really only doing what they want to do. This is true for many who consider themselves Christians. Our lives may be based on an entirely false premise or a premise with which we are not consistent. It is important then what premise I use for determining my life's activities. This assumes that I live consistently with what I claim to be the 'premise' for my life.

C. S. Lewis in his book *Mere Christianity* relates the fact that all of us recognize that there is a standard of conduct that exists above and beyond anything that man has established. If this were not the case, we would not accuse anyone of acting unfairly, as if we expected them to adhere to a high common standard, known by all. Fraudulent accounting practices in business, insider trading, and such things are quickly recognized by all as wrong, and we rightly condemned such actions. If such a standard did not exist, we would not try to hold anyone to it. This brings us to two facts about our makeup that is recognized by almost everyone. First, there is a standard of conduct recognized by society at large to which one's behavior should be consistent. Second, all have, at one time or another, failed to live up to this commonly accepted standard. These things we know within ourselves. This confirms two more things about our makeup. One, there is a basic knowledge of right and wrong within each of us. Two, there is a nature within each of us that causes us to fail to be consistent with this standard. When we fail to live up to the standard (read do evil), we do not attack the standard; we just explain why we had a 'reason' not to adhere to the standard in this specific case, and in every case in which we choose not to follow the standard, which we all know instinctively.

Those who will not acknowledge the above will also refuse to recognize their participation, as such, but which the rest of us recognize immediately. People who refuse to recognize this knowledge and nature do so because of the further conclusions that must be made. A nature to do evil cannot develop from physical evolution, because evil is not a physical thing. Evil is carried out in the physical realm but starts within our minds from a desire, which is 'nonphysical' in itself. Evil requires a nonphysical explanation which surpasses the physical world of time, space, and matter into a spiritual reality. Such an admission is too close to a position of 'there may be a God' and, therefore, too close to destroying the basic premise that 'there is no God', with the supposed moral (read immoral) freedom that results from that premise.

There are many reasons that make 'there is no God' a more comfortable position with which to live. While the above does not prove the existence of God, it should cause the honest thinker to at least consider the possibility. To recognize the spiritual or nonphysical part of the human being has been forced onto the evolutionary thinker. Evolutionists are now trying to determine if the physical, chemical, and electrical processes within the brain can produce a nonmaterial nature. Evolutionists are addressing this, because it is now obvious that there is a spiritual reality for the human being. You will read more about this in newspapers and magazines in the future. Evolutionists (those who say there is no God) will never be able to prove such a thing, but it will give them shelter to remain with their first premise, 'there is no God'.

Furthermore, has there ever been proof that God does not exist? Has there ever been a person so omniscience that he could make such a statement? Where then did such a statement originate? It started in the heart of men who refuse to acknowledge the complexity and marvel of the created universe. God's pronouncement through the Apostle Paul states,

"For since the creation of the world God's invisible qualities—his eternal power and divine nature—have been clearly seen, being understood from what has been made, so that men are without excuse" (Romans 1:20). God goes on to explain that the people do not acknowledge these two invisible qualities of God because of their wickedness. That computes! The created cosmos is one of God's most powerful proofs that he exists. But who will believe it? Certainly not the wicked! The extremely complex DNA molecule with billions of bits of information on how the human being is designed and built demands a designer of godly capability and wisdom.

The resurrection of Christ from the dead is another powerful proof that God exists! Who will consider such a thing, the coming back from the dead? Who will acknowledge the spiritual side to the human being, above all animals, who knows right from wrong, good and evil? What is needed to be sure of the existence of God? Must you meet him face to face? Scripture says that all will meet Christ face to face and kneel before him and will confess that he is the God of Heaven. But, if it is only then that you realize who he is and that he does in fact exist, it will be of no comfort. Only judgment for living with a premise that 'there is no God' will be made.

Jesus, when he was before Pilate, acknowledged who he was and stated, *"Everyone on the side of truth listens to me"* (John 18:37). This is a fantastic statement! Think of the conclusions that are very simple to make when you use this statement as the premise of your thinking. Let us look at some of the conclusions with the following premise: "Everyone on the side of truth listens to Christ."

1. Those who are not on the side of truth will not listen to Christ.
2. If you are not on the side of truth, you must be for a lie.
3. If you are a liar, the Scripture states that you are like your spiritual Father the Devil, who is a liar and the father of lies (including your lies). (John 8:44).
4. If you deny the two invisible qualities that creation shows concerning the Creator God, you are not only a liar, but also a wicked person. (Romans 1:18-20).
5. Evolutionist denies God, i.e., those two invisible qualities that Creation demonstrates about God, therefore, evolutionists are liars, and they also must be wicked. (Make sure you are keeping the correct premise and do not lie to yourself).
6. Evolutionists do not believe in God, and they do not listen to Christ, all because they are liars and are wicked.

This exercise could go on for a long time, but other conclusions need to be made. It is the evolutionists who have, in the present time, entered into the thinking of man that 'God does not exist'. Their position has resonated well with the thinking of a corrupt human mind that also desires to live by a lie and who has a wicked heart. This is to say that, in the natural state, humankind desires to live with an immoral lifestyle and to 'hope' that there will not be a judgment against their wickedness. If they would take an 'honest' (truthful) moment of consideration, they would realize deep down within their own knowledge that they are trying to live a lie. That is their choice—that is their 'freedom of choice'. The exceedingly sad thing, for them, is that while they can freely live this way, they do not have the ability to determine the consequences of that choice. While Creation does not fully explain what the Creator God of Heaven is like—the Scriptures do. If you are on the side of truth, you will listen to Christ, who is the Word of God in the flesh (John 1:1-4; 14).

The very wealthy man who would give money to someone to prove to him that 'God exists' need only be on the side of truth and listen to Christ. The cost to him for doing that will be well worth it, even if not in terms of money.

So, what is the premise for your life? What side do you choose? Are you interested in the existence of the God of Heaven? Are you interested in what acknowledging the existence of God can mean to you? If you would listen to Christ, this is what he said, *"Now this is eternal life: that they may know you, the only true God, and Jesus Christ, whom you have sent"* (John 17:3).

With the premise that 'God exists', you can not only know God and Jesus Christ, but also have eternal life!

Chapter 2

~ What about Evil ~

A question was asked of me: "What is your understanding of evil as it exists in the world?" My short answer was: "Evil is very real, and it is killing a lot of people with eternal consequences!!"

The source of evil and the understanding of it in the world are addressed in as many ways as there are various 'religions' in the world. I address it from the Christian viewpoint, because I am a Christian. In Isaiah 45:7 we read, *"I* (God) *form the light, and create darkness: I make peace, and create evil: I, the Lord, do all these things."* (KJV). Another translation puts it this way,

"I form the light and create darkness, I bring prosperity and create disaster; I, the Lord, do all these things." (NIV) The NIV translation seems more accurate, even though you may consider disaster the same as evil and not a fitting thing for God to do.

Habakkuk certainly felt this way. Habakkuk 1:13, in speaking to God, says, *"Your eyes are too pure to look on evil; you cannot tolerate wrong."* God told Habakkuk earlier (Habakkuk 1:5b), *"For I am going to do something in your days that you would not believe, even if you were told."* God went on to say that he was raising up the Babylonians in judgment against Judah. It was certainly a disaster for Judah, which God caused. Did any evil occur during the Babylonian invasion and the conquering of Judah? Absolutely! God then judged the Babylonians for their evil, just as he had judged Judah for its evil. God created disasters on many occasions in judgment against sin (evil); the 'flood' during the days of Noah is a well-known example.

Evil is not just the absence of 'good', as some try to explain, using the fact of opposites, such as, there is no such 'thing' as cold. Cold, thus, is the absence of heat, not something of itself. 'Hate' may be considered the opposite of love. But hate is more than just the absence of love; hate is active of itself. Darkness is the absence of light, again, not something of itself. While the Scripture uses physical darkness to represent sin and evil, sin and evil are personal and of the spiritual realm even though they manifest into the physical realm. To continue this thought, 'light' represents holiness and righteousness in the Scripture, which is also personal and of the spiritual realm, yet manifests itself in the physical realm. Evil, far from being just the absence of 'good', is active of itself. Because both hate and evil are active on their own, they are personal and intentional. While hate is the opposite of love, hate in action is the 'perversion' of love. Likewise, evil is the opposite of good, yet is, in fact, the perversion of what is good.

We should all be familiar with the fall of Lucifer (Ezekiel 28:11-19; Isaiah 14:12-20), who is now the personification of evil, because he is dedicated to the 'perversion' of all that God has made, which is Good. We read in Genesis 1:31, *"God saw all that he made, and it was very good."* Lucifer, a fallen angel and now called the Devil and our Adversary, is also the committed adversary of God and is in the process of trying to pervert and destroy all the good things that God created, including humankind. The consequence of Satan's success results in perverting 'good' into 'evil', which is known as sin. God judges all sin with death to the sinner unless forgiven in Christ Jesus. Death is not the annihilation into nothingness but rather a separation from God, who is totally righteous, into a place of judgment and suffering according to the sin or perversion committed. God's anger burns against evil (sin) forever, so the punishment for evil (sin) lasts forever, be it against man or angel. (Don't stop reading at this point!).

God created humankind with a great number of 'needs.' This includes physical needs, emotional needs, spiritual needs, etc. God created sex, for example, and he established the boundaries in which he would bless (meet) the sexual needs (desires) for humankind. Sex is to be enjoyed in a holy and sacred union between a husband and wife (one man and one woman) bonded and committed to each other in holy marriage. We are only too familiar with the sexual perversions that now exist because of Satanic, and sin nature, perversions of God's gift and his instructions for holiness and purity. Christ is to meet every need that he created within humankind—without exceptions! (Ephesians 1:22). Evil is the attempt, prompted and encouraged by Satan and our own sin natures, to meet our needs outside of Christ Jesus and the boundaries that he has established for holy and righteous behavior. To continue the example, Satan and our own sin nature promise 'great sex' in a perverted way. The evil promise is 'free sex' without cost or consequence. But the reality is emotional, psychological, and physical costs and the destruction of our own personality and honor and integrity and joy. Many learn this only at great cost.

The disasters that God, in his wisdom and power, sovereignty and righteousness, brings about are examples for people to observe, fear, and shun. They are to turn to him for true fulfillment of needs by his grace, love, forgiveness, provision and eternal life through Christ Jesus. Evil has had great success in the world, but we do not need to become a casualty of its horror. We will find victory over evil only in Christ.

One day in the future God will put an end to all evil and will punish all evil things that have been done and all evil people. There are those, who are evil themselves, who would have us believe that God is a harsh and an unloving master. The parable of the talents addresses this attitude. In the parable of the talents, three servants were entrusted by their master with money to use and invest while he was away. The first two servants were faithful and responsible and gained more money through their individual efforts. The third servant buried the money that his master gave him to use and justified his actions by saying, "Master", he said, "I knew that you are a hard man, harvesting where you have not sown and gathering where you have not scattered seed. So I was afraid and went out and hid your talent in the ground. See, here is what belongs to you" (Matthew 25:24-25). Reading the rest of parable shows that what the third servant said was an unacceptable way to behave.

Far from being harsh and unloving when judging and punishing all sins and evil, God will show grace and mercy to those who come to him for grace and forgiveness. You can be sure that all sin and evil will be paid for in full. Those, however, who come to Christ in humility will find their evil and sin, can be forgiven, paid for by Christ himself when he was crucified for us on the Cross of Calvary. Those who do not seek forgiveness will continue to experience the destruction that sin causes and be eternally separated from the loving God of heaven. We have the freedom to choose how we are going to live—God will respect that. We, however, do not have the freedom to choose the consequences that God has established for those who choose to continue to love a sinful life. God has the complete freedom to establish the condition that "sin will in nowise enter into heaven". *"Nothing impure will ever enter it* (heaven), *nor will anyone who does what is shameful or deceitful, but only those whose names are written in the Lamb's book of life"* (Revelation 21:27).

Does evil exist? Yes, it does, even in our own heart (sin nature). Is evil destructive? Yes, it will destroy even our own soul and spirit! Is there a solution concerning evil? Yes, there is. Evil is to be judged and punished. The personifications of evil (men and angels) will be put to death. The sin nature must be put to death, either with Christ on the cross (Romans 6:6) or taken with you into the 'second death', the 'lake of fire', which lasts forever. (Revelation 20:15). It is not hard to know the right thing to do.

Chapter 3

~ Origin of Humanity ~

It is of eternal importance that we settle in our minds the origin of humanity and to correctly understand the condition and need of humankind for divine grace.

~ Part One ~

There are two basic world views as to the origin of humankind. The first view to consider is that of the evolutionist. The evolutionist 'theory' (theory, because it has never been proven) claims that humans developed from lower life forms through vertical (improved) genetic mutations within the DNA molecule (deoxyribonucleic acid).[1] Positive (vertical) mutations or improved genetic segments of the DNA molecule have never been observed in nature, nor demonstrated in a lab, even where intelligent manipulation is involved. Gene splicing or additions cannot be considered 'normal' positive mutations. To demonstrate this point, I gave one of my biology classes an opportunity to gain extra credit points. They could earn 'one point' for each 'negative' genetic mutation and 'fifty credit points' for each 'positive' genetic mutation that could be found. The students searched biology books, went 'online', called doctors that they knew and took their full two weeks for the assignment searching for 'positive' mutations.

Not one positive mutation could be discovered! One student did offer the possibility that 'six toes' on each foot might be considered a positive mutation. Many negative mutations were found and listed for extra credit points, but no positive mutations were able to be found. The biology book spoke of positive mutations but did not 'bother' to name any. This is not offered as proof positive for the absence of positive mutations but is an antidotal example of what is presently known within genetic knowledge and information.

Due to the extremely long amounts of time supposably necessary in the 'evolutionary' process, normal scientific processes and methods cannot be used to verify evolution. Scientific methods, such as observing and collecting data, measuring and organizing data, classifying, hypothesizing, predicting, experimenting and analyzing new data, inferring, and modeling data, cannot be accomplished because of long time frames involved. It would be similar to analyzing the cross section of a dead cow through the belly and then telling all there is to know about cattle and the history of cattle—it cannot be done. A normal human lifespan would only amount to a 'snapshot' of observable scientific information. It is only 'hypothesizing' that can be done without 'real time' experimentation. In this, the hypothesizing only reflects a philosophy of what is thought to have happened, or to have occurred. As I will address later, even the fossil record, which covers an extended period of time, does not confirm evolution but indicates 'special creation' instead. An additional problem that the evolutionist cannot explain is the source of 'life' and how it came into existence. They know what is 'necessary' for life but cannot show how it came into being—they can only 'hypothesize' what 'must' have happened for life to have occurred. Biogenesis, right out of the biology book, simply states the 'life' comes from pre-existing 'life'. 'Life' cannot be produced from 'nonliving' things—no matter how much 'time' is given. This is a 'real' problem for evolutionists.

I attended the U. S. Air Force aircraft accident investigation school at the University of Southern California. We would address past aircraft accidents that had occurred unobserved and try to discover from wreckage distribution and condition what caused the accident and how events occurred all the way to the crash site and beyond. Investigating aircraft accidents is much simpler than discovering the 'facts' of the beginning of the universe or human origins—but is similar in many ways. Discovery of, or locating, the 'black box' which records instrument readings during the accident helps immensely, but not all aircraft that crash have black boxes. Sometimes all that is available are the 'facts' that are observable at the crash scene. Sometimes weather conditions, etc., are available—sometimes not. Many things are searched out to determine what happened, including the wreckage itself or 'eyewitness' that might be available. Most times, the causes of crashes can be accurately determined, but there are times when only what we 'think' most likely happened becomes our conclusion.

Scientific methods do not lend themselves well to 'one-time events'. Creation or events that have not been scientifically recorded at the time of occurrence, or have not been observed, can be especially hard to understand. Basic 'facts' are the same for all who address the event. In the training process of aircraft accident investigation, two or three teams of student investigators would be assigned to study one accident scene. After investigations were completed, comparisons of student determinations with the results of the 'official' investigation and determination of the accident would be made. At times it was a real 'learning process'.

In the case of 'creation', the facts are the same for everyone. No human was there to observe what happened. We can only take the present 'physical' evidence and use our best judgment as to when and what happened. In this process, we use the best science that we can. In determining what happened to cause what we presently observe of the 'heavens and the earth', there are two basic investigation teams. Both teams have a premise from which they are making their investigation. One team has a premise that there was no 'supernatural' involvement in bringing about what is presently observed. The other team has a premise that there 'was an eyewitness' who not only recorded what happened (not necessarily scientifically) but was personally involved with what happened at the time, and is still involved today, and will be involved in future events. Each team is reporting to you.

The results of aircraft accident investigations are important in order to determine what action, if any, must be taken in order to make flying safer for those who fly, as well as for those who are on the ground. It is, also, important to you what each of the teams investigating the 'heavens and the earth' report. The results of both reports are very different, and their different conclusions will affect you differently—but very significantly. The assumption is that the best science considered effective is used during the investigation, but the one team who will check out the 'eyewitness' account of an event generally has the better chance of solving what happened, especially if the 'eyewitness' is credible.

Another factor to consider is that the motives of investigators can obscure or produce incorrect results, if allowed to go uncorrected. I was assigned to an accident investigation board which involved a commanding general officer of an Air Force major command. The general had landed his aircraft during thunderstorms in the area, which included rain on the runway where he landed. The general skidded off the runway into the soft dirt along the runway. The aircraft was severely damaged and a fuel leak was caused, but without a fire. The general officer had some of his staff (also generals) with him and could have killed himself and most of the command staff.

A junior officer of the investigation team suggested we consider the weather at the time as the cause of the accident and, thus, protect the general officer from any embarrassment that might arise from the investigation. The suggestion was considered because ranking officers can have an affect on career opportunities. I refused the suggestion, in part, because I was representing the Air Weather Service as the weather officer on the investigation board. Integrity required the real cause to be discovered. The general officer was found responsible for the accident, because he did not let the instructor pilot who was with him land the aircraft under adverse weather conditions. General officers do not fly enough to remain proficient and, therefore, are required to fly with a highly qualified and current pilot (read instructor pilot). Due to the passengers on board and the fact that the General insisted on landing in adverse conditions, the Joint Chiefs of Staff gave him a personal, written reprimand. The Air Weather Service had performed their duties completely and professionally.

The investigation board, together, rejected the earlier suggestion and all members of the board worked very well together, including the young officer. The point is not all motives of all investigations and investigators are pure. This goes for political investigations, as well. Personal values are important, but cannot be assumed pure—some people are more than willing to report a lie. Evolutionists, whom society has 'honored' for their 'statements of investigation' about evolution, may need to be reprimanded rather than accepted.

It must be concluded that evolution is, in great part, philosophical and not science, which it claims to totally be. All scientists involved in this effort have the same 'physical facts' to work with but do not come up with the same explanations as to what actually happened. For the evolutionists, it is mostly 'theory' and 'conjecture', even using as much science as possible. This is said because with the science used and available, it is not possible to 'prove' what happened at the 'beginning'. I am being generous in allowing the above to be what the evolutionist sincerely 'thinks' happened. Since the premise of evolutionary thinking is that 'there is no creator God', the above is really what the evolutionary thinker 'thinks' must have happened according to his operational premise that there 'is no God'. If anything goes against their 'theory' of evolution and points to creation, that information is rejected and denied 'out of hand', simply because it goes against the evolutionist's basic premise. For those evolutionists who really know better but want to 'live' as if there were no God of Heaven who judges their 'morality', the refusal to acknowledge what is known of modern genetics results in his doing whatever he thinks he can pass off as fact to uninformed people, who also like the premise that 'there is no God'. He finds that he is 'pleasing' a very large number of people, who are quite happy with his premise.

The double helix structure of the DNA molecule was first described in 1953 by James Watson and Francis Crick. Watson and Crick proposed how the DNA helix would separate into two complementary strands of DNA to form a template, or mold, upon which two new strands of DNA would be exactly replicated—without error.[2] Research later proved this to be exactly what happens with an accuracy rate of one error per billions of replication.[3] The process does not allow for new gene segments, i.e. improved (vertical) genetic material. The entire process of replication occurs with great accuracy. The cell also has a built-in 'proofreading' function, preformed by enzymes or proteins, depending on the organism. So the DNA molecule has a mechanism for repair.[4] Damage to human cells can be caused by several things; body heat, radiation, chemicals, and other factors can damage the DNA molecule.[5] A group of 20 or more repair enzymes recognizes and removes damaged nucleotides and replaces them with new ones, thus ensuring the accurate replication of new DNA.[6] One must realize that all of this is 'current science' and is in direct opposition to the proposed evolutionary process, because this prevents new or vertical development of the DNA.

There are genetic mutations to the DNA molecule, but they are never positive mutations. All known genetic mutations are harmful, resulting from some kind of damage. Most mutations are lethal mutations, and some are benign, at best. If one questions this, just go to the Internet and search out 'positive mutations'. There are thousands of negative mutations. Sickle-cell disease, Huntington disease, hereditary cancers, diabetes, hemophilia, Down's syndrome, color blindness, Turner 's syndrome and Cystic Fibrosis are just a few of the harmful mutations. Evolutionists are so bankrupt for positive mutations that they ingeniously state that Sickle-cell disease, which usually results in death, has a side effect that those with the disease are not affected by malaria. The victim may not get malaria but will likely die with the Sickle-cell disease.[7] If this is an example of a positive mutation; the theory of evolution is in serious trouble.

Also, stem cell research is not to redesign or improve the DNA helix but only to provide genetic repair of cells back to an original state. Gene splicing cannot be considered "blind random chance", because the process is under 'intelligent design' or 'genetic engineering' and, therefore, not to be considered equivalent to an imagined natural positive mutation. It needs to be understood that once the DNA strand has been damaged it will replicate itself with that genetic damage.

The human DNA contains many genes. A **gene** is the segment of DNA on a chromosome that controls a particular hereditary trait. Chromosomes occur in pairs and genes occur in pairs. A contrasting form of a gene is called an **allele.** Alleles are either dominant or recessive, which means, if dominant, they will express themselves as a **phenotype,** which manifests in external appearance, or, if recessive, they will not show up as a physical characteristic. The genetic makeup of an organism is its **genotype,** and the external appearance of an organism is its **phenotype.**[8] The various colors of skin, hair, and eyes, or whether a person is tall, medium, or short, etc, etc, are all included in the multiple alleles of the human DNA. A particular population could go from short and dark-headed to tall and blond-headed with the same strand of human DNA. This is not evolution in the classical sense but rather an expression of dominant alleles within the population's normal DNA. Some have called this 'micro evolution', but there is no additional genetic material (genotype) to the human DNA added or taken away but only a change in phenotype through the expression of dominant alleles. Human DNA has not been improved since the first human was created. The original human DNA strand was perfect at the very beginning and has only deteriorated or undergone destruction through negative mutations. In fact, with all the negative mutations (thousands of them), our present DNA has been so damaged that as time goes on the human race will be destroyed through continued negative mutations within our DNA.[9]

One example of a change in phenotype is the incident of the Tower of Babel recorded in Genesis 11, where *"the Lord confused the language of the whole world" and " . . . scattered them over the face of the whole earth"* (Verse 9). Humans were divided from each other according to language, which resulted in dominant alleles to be expressed within the various groups, causing a particular phenotype within that group. Various groups ended up expressing different phenotypes, yet all were very much in possession of the same human DNA.

Furthermore, each species has a distinct DNA. All the different kinds of dogs possess the same 'dog DNA'. All the different kinds of cows possess the same 'cow DNA'. All the different kinds of horses possess the same 'horse DNA'. The different kinds (species) of DNA molecules do not 'crossover' naturally.[10] If a male donkey is crossed with a female horse, the result is a 'sterile' mule that cannot reproduce. If a male horse is crossed with a female donkey you get a 'sterile' hinny that can not reproduce. This all speaks directly against the possibility of the proposed evolutionary process of the generation of many 'species' from one DNA source. This is to say, modern science itself demonstrates the impossibility of genetic evolution as proposed by evolutionists.

Marvin L. Lubenow (Professor of Bible and Apologetics, Christian Heritage College, El Cajon, California) in his book *"Bones of contention"* demonstrates the failure of the 'human fossil record' to verify the contention that humans developed from lower life forms. The human fossil record is strongly supportive of the concept of Special Creation. To the evolutionist, the Australopithecines are the pre-ancestor of the human being. The Australopithecine is nothing more than an extinct primate. The fossil record shows that modern human fossils appeared in the fossil record (even using the evolutionist time frames) before the Australopithecines and lived as contemporaries with the Australopithecines throughout all of Australopithecine history to prove that they had nothing to do with human origins. Archeological evidence also demonstrates that the distinction between *Homo erectus* and *Homo sapiens* (modern humans for the evolutionist) is an artificial one. Stone tools were once considered an almost independent confirmation of the evolutionary development of the human mind, i.e., *Homo habilis* to *Homo erectus* to *Homo Sapien.* Things are different now. Almost every basic style of tool has been found with almost every category of human fossil material. Stringer (Chris Stringer, British Museum— Natural History) and Grun (Rainer Grun, *Nature*) write: "The simplistic equation of hominids and technologies in Europe has thus been abandoned." [11]

Modern human fossils were contemporary to the 'supposed forerunners' of modern humans—which proves that they could not have had any 'evolutionary' part in the modern human. Thus, the human fossil record disproves evolution as well as modern genetic science.

~ *Part Two* ~

The second world view of the origin of humanity (and every thing else) is that contained in the Scriptural account of 'the heavens and the earth' and man's special creation by the Eternal God of Heaven. This is the 'eyewitness' account as mentioned above. It is up to you to determine the 'creditability' of this witness for yourself. This is the only account that explains the basic questions: "Who am I?", "What is my purpose?", and "What is to happen to me?" The existence of God is hard for many to understand and accept. The Apostle Paul addresses a common excuse that many would try to use.

> *The wrath of God is being revealed from heaven against all the godlessness and wickedness of men who suppress the truth by their wickedness, since what may be known about God is plain to them, because God has made it plain to them. For since the creation of the world God's invisible qualities—his eternal power and divine nature—have been clearly seen, being understood from what has been made, so that men are without excuse.* Romans 1:18-20

Paul, under the inspiration of the Spirit of God, is simply telling us that all we have to do is to look around us at all of creation and conclude in our minds that someone very powerful and very intelligent had to have created all that we can see. Creation is 'something' and 'something' cannot come from 'nothing', especially with that 'something' containing the 'mass' of the universe.

The only people who think 'something' can come from 'nothing' that contains the total 'mass' of the universe are those who live with the premise that 'there is no God'. The evolutionists, in addressing the 'big bang', can not go back to a point in time that equals 'zero' or before. There is nothing in the evolutionist's philosophy or experience that can account for the mass of the universe coming into being in the way they describe the 'big bang.'

God informs us that people who can look at the heavens and not see the need for a creator are 'godless' and 'wicked' and 'suppress the truth'. I might add that they also deny 'current genetic knowledge' and the 'truth of the human fossil record.' Evolutionists do not put the complete fossil record on 'one' chart, because it would show the conclusions reached by Marvin Lubenow.

If people are unable to see the need for a powerful and an intelligent creator when they look around, then they should consider the extent of their 'wickedness' and their desire to suppress the 'truth' that does not fit with their desired basic premise for life.

I will be the first to confirm that looking at the universe does not tell us all about God, but it does tell us of his existence; Scripture tells us everything else that we need to know about God and about ourselves.

Scripture tells us that Adam and Eve were the first humans and were a special creation (Genesis 1:26) in the image and likeness of God. God is spirit (John 4:24), and man is both spirit and flesh and blood. God is spirit only, and to be created in his image and likeness is to be created in his spiritual likeness—not a physical likeness. God is holy (Leviticus 19:2b), and to be made in the image and likeness of God is to be created holy. We were not created with any of God's other attributes. Because we were created to be holy like God, we were created to use all of our talents and capabilities in a 'moral' (read holy) manner. We read in Genesis Chapter 3 of the disobedience to God by Adam and Eve, resulting in death: spiritual death (separation from God and into spiritual un-holiness) immediately and physical death eventually. Adam and Eve became unholy like the Devil who deceived Eve to sin and led Adam to sin. Adam and Eve received a nature to continue to sin, and that nature has been passed on to all descendents of Adam and Eve (all of us). Scripture tells us that we are slaves to sin and are not capable, on our own, not to sin. (Romans 6:6; 7:14-17). Left to our own abilities we would become increasingly sinful (Ephesians 4:17-19). The Apostle Paul summarizes the human condition. *"As it is written, 'There is no one righteous* (holy), *not even one; there is no one who understands, no one who seeks God. All have turned away, they have together become worthless; there is no one who does good, not even one'"* (Romans 3:10-12). Among those who have turned away are those evolutionists who have denied God's existence and who have turned away because of their morals.

It was while we were in this deplorable condition that Christ died for our sins. *"You see, at just the right time, when we were still powerless, Christ died for the ungodly"* (Romans 5:6).

Humanity is not able to recover from sin by our own 'works.' We cannot be 'good' enough by our own works or effort to become acceptable as 'holy' (righteous) before God. If Christ had not died to pay for our sins and to rescue us from our 'spiritual death', we would be forever lost. God had to intervene to help us. Christ provided the 'way' to salvation, and it is the Holy Spirit that applies salvation to us and enables us to become saved and to live a victorious life before God the Father. This is explained in more detail in the chapter "Why So Many Lost?"

An understanding of the 'Origin of Humanity' and the 'future' of humanity is very important—it is not something for you to leave to someone else to decide for you. You are individually responsible for responding to the 'truth' (facts) and for your 'calling' for repentance from sin (immorality) by the Creator God of Heaven who desires to cleanse you of your sin and to bless you through 'Christ' as your Savior and Redeemer, and who has the 'gift' of eternal life for you.

Endnotes

[1] Albert Towle, ed., "Mutations," Modern Biology – Teacher's Edition (Chicago: Holt, Rinehart and Winston, 1989) 163.
[2] Towle, "The Double Helix," 114-115.
[3] Towle, "Accuracy and Repair," 116.
[4] Towle, 116-117.
[5] Towle, 116-117.
[6] Towle, 116-117.
[7] "Can genetic mutations produce positive changes in living," Mutations: Evolution or Degeneration, 6, 23 March 2011 <*http://christiananswers.net/q-eden/genetic-mutations.html*>.
[8] Towle, "Chromosomes and Genes," 152-153.
[9] "Can genetic mutations produce positive changes in living," Mutations: Evolution or Degeneration, 8, 23 March 2011 <*http://christiananswers.net/q-eden/genetic-mutations.html*>.
[10] Towle, "Hybridization," 192.
[11] Chris B. Stringer and Rainer Grun, "Time for the last Neanderthals," Nature, 351 (27 June 1991) 701.

Chapter 4

~ The Fruit Tree ~

People do not seem to like considering the fruit of the tree that Eve found so interesting in the Garden of Eden. The fruit of the tree was the 'knowledge of good and evil.' This fruit represented more than just the natural fruit that a tree would normally produce. The fruit of this particular tree, when eaten in disobedience to the direct command of God to Adam, would take away the innocence of ignorance about what is good and what is evil, replacing that carefree innocence with a new personal responsibility to do what is good and to refrain from that which is evil. (Job 1:8). In a sense, just as the serpent promised Eve, eating the fruit did make them like God in that God knows the difference between good and evil, and now, so did Adam and Eve. However, it also made them like the Devil who also has the knowledge of good and evil. While God does only good, Satan does only evil. Mankind now had the potential for doing both.

Doing good and refraining from evil would be hard enough for Adam and Eve to do without any further complications, but that did not come near to being the sum of their problems because of their disobedience to God. Not only did they now know the difference between good and evil but also they now became like Satan, their new Spiritual Father (John 8:44) – with a spiritual nature to keep doing evil. (Romans 3:10-20). The Apostle Paul stated the problem this way: *"Don't you know that when you offer yourselves to someone to obey him as slaves, you are slaves to the one whom you obey—whether you are slaves to sin* (disobedience to God, or evil), ***which leads to death**, or to obedience* (good) *which leads to righteousness?"* (Romans 6:16). (Emphasis is mine.) This is why God told Adam that when he ate of the fruit of the tree that he would surely die—which he did. (Genesis 2:17).

Christ, when conversing with the Jews who were persecuting him, further defined mankind's relationship with Satan. *"If God were your Father, you would love me, for I came from God and now am here. I have not come on my own; but he sent me. Why is my language not clear to you? Because you are unable to hear what I say. You belong to your father, the devil, and you want to carry out your father's desire. He was a murderer from the beginning, not holding to the truth, for there is no truth in him"* (John 8:42-44).

This should help us understand that even the Jews who knew all about God did not have God as their spiritual Father, but the Devil was, in fact, their spiritual Father. The Scripture is, of course, speaking in the spiritual sense and not in a physical sense. Christ stated that they wanted to carry out their father's desire. They wanted to do what the Devil wanted them to do, because they had the Devil's very nature to do evil. The Jews, in fact, wanted to murder Jesus (John 8:59), which they ended up doing.

Sin and death entered into the world for all humankind through Adam's sin of disobedience in eating the fruit of "the tree of the knowledge of good and evil". Did Adam and Eve understand all of this 'theology' when they disobeyed God? I do not think so. The Scriptures do not indicate anywhere that Adam and Eve understood all the ramifications of their disobedience, and Eve did not mention any of these things when talking to the Devil in the garden (Genesis 3). From God's point of view if he told them not to eat of the tree of the Knowledge of Good and Evil—that was all they needed to know! God works the same way with us. When God tells us not to be sexually immoral—he does not bother to tell us of all the heartache, emotional suffering, physical disease, etc, that accompanies sexual immorality; he considers it enough that he told us not to be sexually immoral and that we should trust him and be obedient to his command. The same goes with all his commands to us. Trust and obey! No explanation needed—signed—your Creator!

It must be noted that our sin nature overpowers us, since we are 'slaves' to our sin nature (Romans 6:6-7) and that by ourselves we are not able to do 'good' all the time, or to refrain from 'evil' all the time. God knows this, and we should realize our condition as well. We are doomed to die physically because of this. We are already dead spiritually in our transgressions and sins (Ephesians 2:1-3), and unless Christ becomes our savior, we will stay in this condition (John 3:17-21). When we understand this, we generally become upset and indignant and think that God is treating us like 'dust on the scales' as Isaiah 40:15 says, *"Surely the nations are like a drop in a bucket, they are regarded as dust on the scales; . . ."* We, as 'dust particles', need to put away our pride and to humble ourselves and accept Christ as our savior and become obedient—even unto death, even as our Lord Jesus did. (Philippians 2:8). If we gave more deference to our Creator and worried less about who we think we are and what we think we aught to have, we would be brought to salvation. Our Creator has chosen to love us with an eternal love, but he is not only our Creator, but also the Lord of justice, as well. We need to be grateful that he is the Lord of love and grace, forgiveness and salvation. (John 3:16).

~The Sin Nature ~

At this point we may say, "Okay, I see how Adam and Eve got their sin nature, but how did I get mine, since I had nothing to do with what they did?" This addresses an additional consequence of Adam and Eve's disobedience in the garden. The Apostle Paul addresses this question in the fifth chapter of his letter to the Romans. Several verses explain what happened. Verse 12: *"Therefore, just as sin entered the world through one man* (Adam), *and death through sin, and in this way death came to all men, because all sinned—";* Verse 16b: *"The judgment followed one sin and brought condemnation* (to all)*";* Verse 18: *Consequently, just as the result of one trespass* (Adam's) *was condemnation for all men";* Verse 19: *"For just as through the disobedience of one man the many were made sinners, . . ."*

We were all made sinners, because Adam's nature to sin was passed on to all of humankind just like the consequence of sin, i.e., death, was passed on to all humankind. Therefore, we became just like Adam by receiving from him a nature to sin, i.e., the sin nature. Remember that our sin nature is not part of our original design when we were created! Our human nature, with which we were created, was stated to be 'very good'. (Genesis 1:31). The spiritual 'human nature' and the spiritual 'sin nature' meld together in a seamless spiritual 'unity' but they are separate natures. However, now for all practical purposes, they work as one nature prone to sin.

Scripture does not directly address how or when the passing of the sin nature occurs, but does so indirectly. Several scriptures are helpful. In Psalm 51:5, King David was inspired to say, *"Surely I was sinful at birth, sinful from the time my mother conceived me.*"To be sinful from the moment of conception would mean that one has a sin nature beginning at the moment of conception. No baby commits a personal sin at the moment of conception, so the only way to be sinful would be to have a sin nature passed on to us at that moment. If a baby receives a sin nature at the moment of conception, there are several options. A baby could receive a sin nature through the father, or the mother, or through both, or from an act of God giving the baby a sin nature at the moment of conception.

While all mankind is born with the sin nature as a result of Adam and Eve eating the forbidden fruit, this is not true of Christ in human form. The Apostle Paul states that Jesus Christ concerning "his human nature was a descendent of David, and who through the Spirit of holiness was declared with power to be the Son of God by his resurrection from the dead" (Romans 1:3). In this, we are to understand that Jesus did not have a sin nature. Though the sin nature is a spiritual thing, Jesus did not receive a sin nature from the Father (God the Father) as part of his spiritual makeup. We also read that a "virgin will be with child and will give birth to a son, and will call him Immanuel" (meaning God with us) (Isaiah 7:14, Matthew 1:22-23). Mary was that virgin, who was the mother of Jesus, and she did not pass on to Jesus a sin nature. It is not impossible that God prevented, supernaturally, such a thing from happening, but the Scriptures do not address such a thing. It would seem reasonable to do that, if that were the case, because it is very specific that she was a virgin, having never been with a male. Neither does scripture state any place that it is God who gives everyone, or anyone, a sin nature at conception. Scripture is very definite that it is through Adam (the male) that many were made sinners, i.e., everyone! While we must be careful with our conclusions, it would seem reasonable that if we become sinners at conception and that Adam has caused 'many' (all) to become sinners that the sin nature is passed to the offspring through the father and not through the mother or from God.

~ *Good and Evil a Law?* ~

The first thing that happened to Adam and Eve after eating of the tree of the Knowledge and Good and Evil was that the eyes of them both were opened, and they realized they were naked. Immediately they sewed fig leaves together to cover their nakedness. (Genesis 3:7). They realized that they were 'naked' and that the condition was 'evil' and not 'good'. Their immediate response was to make coverings for themselves. I would press this point and ask what this has to say about those who promote nudity, or set up nudist camps, or establish nude beaches, etc., or who attend or participate in such activities? This truth was immediately known by our first parents—and it is 'innate' to us as well, but there are those who respond to their sinful nature and deny that such is true. What should this say to us?

When anyone gets into legal trouble, one of the first things addressed is whether or not the individual understands right from wrong (read good from evil). Knowing right from wrong is something that became innate within a human being even as the sin nature became part of us. Unless people have become so mentally deficient that they really cannot determine reality (right from wrong), then they are responsible to do what is right (good) and refrain from wrong (evil). When John Hinckley shot President Ronald Regan, it took our institutions a year to determine that Hinckley, in fact, knew the difference between right and wrong (read good from evil), and, therefore, was able to stand trial for the evil that he had committed. How many try to fain insanity as an excuse for committing evil? Our sin nature is what causes us to do evil (read sin). Scripture tells us that we become more and more depraved to do evil, unless something intervenes to slow the process down, or to reverse the process (Ephesians 4:18-19). If left totally unchecked, we would become totally depraved. (Romans 3:9-20; Ephesians 4:17-19). Most people are somewhere in between: sometimes doing the right thing and sometimes doing the evil thing. The Apostle Paul addresses this in the second chapter of his letter to the Romans.

> *All who sin apart from the law* (Mosaic Law) *will also perish apart from the law* (Mosaic Law), *and all who sin under the law* (Mosaic Law) *will be judged by the law* (Mosaic Law). *For it is not those who hear the law* (Mosaic Law) *who are righteous in God's sight, but it is those who obey the law* (Mosaic Law) *who will be declared righteous. (Indeed, when Gentiles, who do not have the law* (Mosaic Law), *do by nature things required by the law* (Mosaic Law), *they are a law* (Natural Law, Knowledge of Good and Evil) *for themselves, even though they do not have the law* (Mosaic Law), *since they show that the requirements of the law* (Mosaic Law) *are written on their hearts, their consciences also bearing witness, and their thoughts now accusing, now even defending them.) This will take place on the day when God will judge men's secrets* (their thoughts and attitudes) *through Jesus Christ, as my gospel declares.* (Romans 2:12-16).

There is much for us to learn from these verses. The Mosaic Law was given to the Jews—not to the Gentiles, and I need to add—and not to the Church. The church (Christians) is under the Law of the Spirit of Life. (Romans 8:2). We learn a lot about God through the Mosaic Law, and we should be very familiar with that law, but we are not under that law, but under Grace, which is the Law of the Spirit of Life. (Romans 6:14).

No Jew will ever be justified by his obedience to the Mosaic Law. (Romans 3:20). All Gentiles are under the Natural Law of the Knowledge of Good and Evil. Not one Gentile will be saved by his obedience to the Natural Law (Romans 2:12), and unless both are saved by grace through faith in Christ (Ephesians 2:8-9), both will perish. The Gentile will be judged by the Natural Law of the Knowledge of Good and Evil. In this age of Grace, Jews and Gentiles are saved in the same manner—by Grace alone through faith. (Ephesians 2:8-9). Christ will judge by searching out the secrets of men's (everyone's) hearts. You may fool me completely in what you know and do not know, or by your outward appearance, but you will not fool your judge—the Lord Jesus Christ.

~ Any Old Testament Gentiles Saved? ~

The short answer to the above question is, yes! The Mosaic Law is not mentioned in the book of Job, but the testimony is that Job was a 'righteous man', i.e., he had eternal life. *"Then the Lord said to Satan, 'Have you considered my servant Job? There is no one on earth like him; he is blameless and upright, a man who fears God and shuns evil'"* (Job 1:8).

Job was righteous on the same basis that Abraham was declared righteous in Genesis 15:6. *"Abram believed the Lord, and he credited it to him as righteousness."* Job believed God, i.e., 'fears God', and while he was not sinless (no one is, except Christ), Job's life was noted as 'blameless and upright, a man who fears God and shuns evil. Job's behavior was very commendable, but that was not the basis for him being considered righteous. Job's friends were anything but helpful to Job; in fact, they were downright ugly to him, yet they believed in God. Many in that era were saved. Many Old Testament Gentiles have been saved on the same basis as Abraham, including people such as Nebuchadnezzar (Daniel 4:34-37). We must remember that Abraham was saved before he became circumcised (Romans 4:1-12). Hebrews 11:4-7 speaks of Abel, Enoch, and Noah who were in the technical sense Gentiles but were also men of faith. Melchizedek the king of Salem and priest of God Most High (Hebrews 7:1) would also fall into this category if he was just a human. There is reason, however, to believe that he may have been Christ himself in a pre-incarnate form, but this study is too short for that discussion. The Old Testament focuses primarily on the Hebrews and was not directed to indicate those Gentiles that God may have dealt with outside of that special nation. It is most probable that most Gentiles did not acknowledge the Creator God of Heaven but were deeply involved in pagan idol worship, which was generally very sensual and immoral. The three wise men that came to worship Christ were Gentiles and most likely came from a line of righteous Gentiles who lived in Babylon and were the product of Daniel's witness to them.

~ *In the Image of God* ~

It is God's plan to restore humankind to its original, created form, one made in the image of God himself. Genesis 1:26 records for us the creation of humankind. *"Then God said, 'Let us make man in our image, in our likeness, and let them rule over the fish of the sea and the birds of the air, over the livestock, over all the earth, and over all the creatures that move along the ground.'"*

Earlier verses in this chapter record the creation of the heavens and the earth, along with everything else that God created in the seven (literal) days of creation. As creator, God would rule over all creation in the same manner that he expected Adam and Eve to start ruling over their assigned duties. Humankind was created in the 'image' and 'likeness' of God, so that they could rule in the same way that God ruled things. If we understand how God rules things, we will understand how Adam and Eve were created in his image and likeness, so that they could rule earthly things like God rules all things.

In order for us to find out how God rules things, we must look at the character and attributes of God. We need to learn who God is and then learn how he does things. To learn of God is best done by looking at the attributes of God and then see if there is an overriding principle (attribute) in how he does things. In looking at the attributes of God, it is too much for this study to go into a great deal about each attribute, so we will only make surface observations about each attribute and compare the attribute to humankind. The attributes mentioned are not taken in any order of importance and will not exhaust our understanding of God.

The attributes of God include that he is omnipresent. God is spirit (John 4:24) and can be everywhere all the time. He is not physical and limited in being at one place at a time. Humankind, being physical, is limited to being at one place at a time. God is omniscient, which means he knows everything. He knows everything from eternity past to eternity future. This is more than most people can mentally comprehend since we are not infinite like God is. We are finite and our knowledge is finite, which is to say very limited—just like our understanding.

God is omnipotent, which is to say that he is all powerful. There is nothing that God cannot do. This is totally unlike humankind. Samson may have been a very strong man, but humankind, and even the strongest angels (including Satan), is no match for the omnipotence of God. God is perfect, without any imperfection, in his faithfulness, goodness, patience, grace, mercy, love, and yes—even his wrath. God is perfect in his holiness. Every attribute that defines who God is, is used and perfected by his holiness. To be holy can be understood in two ways. First, to be holy is to do all things right—never to do anything wrong. Second, to be holy can be understood to mean to be set apart for God's purpose. God's holiness is to be understood by the first understanding—God does everything right—all the time!

Can you imagine total power that is not guided by holiness? Can you imagine total knowledge not guided by holiness? Can you imagine ruling things without holiness? Can you imagine any other attribute of either God or humankind not controlled by holiness? Leviticus 19:2 states, *"Be holy because I, the Lord your God, am holy."* Peter quotes this very scripture in 1 Peter 1:16: *"Be holy because I am holy."* (Also Leviticus 11:44-45; 20:7).

God commands us to be holy, because he is holy. He also commands us to be faithful, good, patient, merciful, to love, to be angry but not to sin in that anger, etc., and in all of these things, we are to let holiness be in control. God's supreme attribute that glorifies all of his other attributes, and which he demands of us, is 'holiness'. We were chosen in Christ before the creation of the world to be holy and blameless in his sight. (Ephesians 1:4). As Christians, it is God's purpose through sanctification to make us holy again—the same way that we were originally created!

Adam and Eve, even in their innocence of good and evil, were created as holy and were to rule all of their assignment in holiness (read moral responsibility). Adam and Eve had moral responsibility, even though innocent of 'good' and 'evil', because God gave them a 'command' to follow, along with a free will to either choose obedience or to rebel. Holiness is a moral characteristic of God and was to be theirs, as well. In holiness, Adam and Eve were to do the 'right' thing and be obedient to God, who created them. They lost their holiness when they sinned and received a sin nature of unholiness, from their new spiritual father—the Devil. (John 8:44). When God draws us to himself to forgive us of our sins and to cleanse us from all unrighteousness, he begins immediately to make us holy and blameless again in all that we are to do. (Ephesians 1:4). This process is called sanctification and starts when we are 'born again' and lasts until we die physically.

Agape love is part of the 'fruit of the Spirit' to be produced in us. Agape love is an attribute of God alone and was not part of human creation, nor is it restored to being a 'natural' part of us even as 'new creations' in Christ. (2 Corinthians 5:17). Agape love is to be produced in us by the indwelling Holy Spirit on a continuous basis—not a one-time empowerment. We must 'abide' in Christ on a continuous basis in order to express all of the fruit of the Spirit. (Galatians 5:22-25, John 15:5). It is also true that without God holiness is not possible, but even after the fall (read disobedience of Adam and Eve) humankind still had a 'moral responsibility' to refrain from 'evil' and to do 'good', But they could not accomplish that on a continuous basis, because they were no longer holy. Human attributes are to be controlled by holiness even as God's attributes are controlled by his holiness.

~ Conclusion ~

God knew everything and purposed everything before anything came into being. Ephesians 1:4 says that God chose us in him (Christ) before the creation of the world. God did not intend the circumstances of the Garden of Eden to continue forever. God did not cause the fall of Lucifer, because God never does anything wrong, but God's plan included everything that happened in the Garden of Eden. God's plans and purposes are unsearchable (Romans 11:33-36) for us, but God has made his will and purpose for each of us able to be known and accomplished. It is not God's purpose to restore things back to what they were in the Garden of Eden. Scripture does not tell us all that we would like to know about heaven and eternity, but it is definitely not going to be a Garden of Eden in a state of ignorance of 'good and evil'. It is God's purpose for us to be a 'Royal Priesthood' to rule and reign with Christ (1 Peter 2:9; Revelation 1:6). This will include 'all wisdom' and not 'ignorance' that would prevent us from judging even angels (1 Corinthians 6:3). Everything that was lost and marred in the

Garden has now been more than repurchased or recovered by the blood of Christ on the Cross; all things will be turned into bright glory in the heavenly realms with Christ as King of Kings and Lord of Lords, not as one walking through the garden in the cool of the day (Genesis 3:8). The Tree of Life will be in heaven (Revelation 22:2), but the Tree of the Knowledge of Good and Evil is gone forever, its fruit no longer available or needed to make us aware of 'good' and 'evil'.

Chapter 5

~ *Why so Many Lost?* ~

The Scripture tells us very plainly that the majority of humans will perish and not make it to heaven (eternal life). *"Enter through the narrow gate. For wide is the gate and broad is the road that leads to destruction, and many enter through it. But small is the gate and narrow the road that leads to life, and only a few find it"* (Matthew 7:13-14). It was the God-man, Jesus Christ, who said these words. How many have already rejected this premise—because they have already rejected the 'small gate' that leads to life—namely Christ! Millions of people who are associated with the world's religions who are not trusting in Christ for salvation are, according to Scripture, lost, and are traveling that broad road.

The Parable of the Sower (Matthew 13:1-9; 18-23) lists many reasons why the 'seed', which is the word of God, is ineffective in so many people. People's hearts are too hardened to accept the word, the word is not able to take root because the heart (mind) is too shallow (read empty), trouble or persecution because of the word causes people to fall away, and the worries of this life and the deceitfulness of wealth choke it out.

The sin nature within us hardens us to the word, because we love to embrace the lusts of our sin nature. Too many people live such shallow lives that they have no desire for commitment to difficult things—no matter how 'good' that would be for them. Many people want to live lives that do not 'cause waves' or draw unloving criticism to themselves; they just concentrate on 'earning a living' to provide for their family in the 'here and now' and do not worry about 'eternity'. Being wealthy in this life seems to promise provisions for all the 'needs' that we will ever have and, therefore, we do not need God. Also, our sin nature, through self-will, promises to provide for every need of the human heart its way, and promises to be more exciting and enjoyable than getting our human needs filled through God's holy and righteous way.

To make a point in passing, it should be noted that the 'fruitfulness' of the 'seed' even in the heart of the believer is not the same for every believer. *"Still other seed fell on good soil* (hearts), *where it produced a crop—a hundred, sixty or thirty times what was sown"* (Matthew 13:8). This fact is consistent with the Parable of the Talents (Matthew 25:14-30), where it is recognized that believers have different abilities. God is pleased with the use of any and all talents for his glory. The servant who buried his master's talent that was given to him was not a 'believing' servant for he did not 'know' the master, nor did he serve the master.

~ *Major Sin Early* ~

Another account of a 'major' sin comes early in the Scriptures, also. Within the very first family, eternal loss was experienced by the very first person to be born into humanity, by his becoming a murderer and living his own self-willed way. Genesis 4 records the events for us. We are told that *"Cain* (the very first person born into humankind) *worked the soil"*, while *"Abel* (the very second person born into humankind) *kept flocks"*. *"In the course of time Cain brought some of the fruits of the soil as an offering to the Lord. But Abel brought fat portions from some of the firstborn of his flock. The Lord looked with favor on Abel and his offering, but on Cain and his offering he did not look with favor. So Cain was very angry, and his face was downcast."*

As we read Genesis, we are left wondering what the problem was between Cain and Abel and their offerings. The Scripture does not explain to us at this point, but all the facts were well known to all those involved at the time. We have to go to other Scripture to fill in the details for ourselves.

We look at Hebrews 11:4 for the first part of our understanding of the problem. *"By faith Abel offered God a better sacrifice than Cain did. By faith he was commended as a righteous man, when God spoke well of his offerings. And by faith he still speaks, even though he is dead."*

Here we are told that Abel was a man of 'faith', which is to say that he believed in God and was obedient to the will of God. Because of this, he was commended as a righteous man. In this, we must recognize that Cain was not a man of 'faith' and that he was not acting in obedience to the will of God and was, therefore, to be considered an unrighteous man. We still lack all the understanding that we want to know about the situation. It is here that some have suggested that Cain's offering was from the ground that had been cursed and was, therefore, an unacceptable offering. This may be true in part, but it is not the complete answer. We read in Leviticus that a "grain" offering, which comes from the 'ground', was part of the worship offerings under the Mosaic Law and was an offering whose aroma was pleasing to the Lord (Leviticus 2).

Reading further in Genesis 4, we learn more. Genesis 4:6-7. *"Then the Lord said to Cain, 'Why are you angry? Why is your face downcast? If you do what is right, will you not be accepted? But if you do not do what is right, sin is crouching at your door; it desires to have you, but you must master it.'"* The Lord himself is talking to Cain, but we do not have a recorded answer from Cain to the Lord. We can answer some questions from what the Lord asked. The Lord's question "Why are you angry?" indicates that Cain did not have a 'real' or 'good' reason to be angry. Genesis 4 goes on to describe how Cain took Abel out into the field and killed him—so Cain must have stayed angry. It is also obvious that Cain's anger, in part, was directed at Abel, which we have yet to discover why.

The Lord God also asked, *"If you do what is right, will you not be accepted?"* In this question, we can know that if Cain had done the 'right' thing, as Abel had done, that he (Cain) would have been every bit as accepted, to God, as Abel had been. It is very evident that Cain did not choose to do the right thing, but had stubbornly insisted to do the thing that he wanted to do, which we must conclude was the wrong thing to do before God.

What can we learn from Abel's involvement in the situation? Are we to understand anything special about Abel? The short answer is, yes! For the answer, we need to go to Luke 11:49-51. The whole scriptural thought from which we are taking our answer includes Luke 11:37-53. Jesus is pronouncing six woes upon the ungodly Pharisees who were pretending to be 'righteous' but who were, in fact, totally 'unrighteous.' They were actually doing the same thing that Cain had done, and they were involved in the same thing that Cain had done—they killed 'prophets'. In our chosen Scripture, Christ says,

> *Because of this, God in his wisdom said, 'I will send them prophets and apostles, some of whom they will kill and others they will persecute.' Therefore this generation will be held responsible for the blood of all the* ***prophets*** *that has been shed since the beginning of the world, from the blood of* ***Abel*** *to the blood of Zechariah, who was killed between the altar and the sanctuary. Yes, I tell you, this generation will be held responsible for it all."* (Luke 11: 49-51) (Emphasis mine).

In this passage, we learn that Abel was a prophet, and we know that his blood was shed by Cain, who acted just as ungodly as the Pharisees in Christ's time, who were instrumental in shedding Christ's blood, as well. Abel was made a prophet to teach God's will. We, too, must learn how to worship and sacrifice to God, following the example of the prophets. Cain's ungodly attitude was focused against his 'younger brother' who was a prophet of God. Cain's attitude was every bit as ungodly as all other ungodly but "religious" pretenders after him. Cain's anger against Abel was murderous. Cain wanted to be 'religious', just like the Pharisees, and like the Pharisees, Cain wanted to be 'religious' on his own terms. Jude, in his letter, describes the situation. Jude, Verse 11b, says: *"Woe to them! They have taken the way of Cain;"* To 'take the way of Cain' is to be 'religious', but to be 'religious' in one's own way. Except for Christianity, all of the various religions of the world want to be 'religious', but to be 'religious' on their own terms. The Apostle Paul speaks of the leaders of all these false religions: *"For such men are false apostles, deceitful workmen, masquerading as apostles of Christ* (or as righteous). *And no wonder, for Satan himself masquerades as an angel of light. It is not surprising, then, if his servants masquerades as servants of righteousness. Their end will be what their actions deserve"* (2 Co. 11: 13-15).

~ *A Religious World* ~

The world is actually very religious, but like Cain, the religious people of the world are religious on their own terms. Buddhism, Christian Science, Mormonism, Druidism, Taoism, Deism, Spiritism, Eckankar, The Way International, Hinduism, Islam, Jehovah's Witnesses, Wicca, New Age Spirituality, Scientology, Shinto, Unification Church, Voodoo, African Traditional Religion, Chinese Traditional, Rastafarianism, Secular Humanism, The Creativity Movement, and such, are all religious but have gone the way of Cain. They are lost as far as any relationship with the God of Heaven is concerned. It is the one resurrected from the dead who said, *"I am the way and the truth and the life. No one comes to the Father except through me"* (John 14:6). None of the above listed religions are trying to get to the Father through Christ of the New Testament (New Covenant). If anyone attempts to reach God by his/her own righteousness, he/she must remember this: God does not grade on the curve! One is totally righteous God's way (Righteous by faith, Romans 1:17; Galatians 3:11; Hebrews 10:38) or is not righteous at all (Galatians 3:10-12). My righteousness has been given to me from the righteous one, who is Christ Jesus my Lord.

People may complain that Christianity is exclusive, and is mean and ugly. My response will be yes, no, and no. Anyone who wants to come to the Father through Christ is more than welcome, and, in fact, that is just what the Holy Spirit is doing in this world, drawing people to Christ. If one's pride and arrogance keeps one from acknowledging one's sin and confessing that sin and receiving the free gift of eternal life from the God of Heaven and from Jesus Christ, who died on the cross to pay for our sins, then that person can be religious the way he/she wants to be religious. However, one should not be fooled: such a 'religious choice' is not living the 'truth' of Scripture nor will such a life lead to heavenly bliss. There are no promises from the God of Heaven, except in Scripture, which promises eternal life, and eternal life is through Jesus Christ, the Son of God (1 John 5:11-12).

~ The Conclusion ~

It was the Lord God himself who worked with Cain to encourage Cain to do the right thing. Abel, as a prophet, was involved as a witness to the 'truth', but God himself intervened and gave Cain every opportunity to do 'what was right'. But, Cain persisted in doing things 'his own way' and to disregard the 'truth' and God's own intervention. God did not kill Cain for murder because such a 'law' did not come into being until after the flood. (Genesis 9:4-6) Cain perished in his own self-will. We are to be witnesses to the 'truth', and God has and continues to intervene by the Holy Spirit in events and in the hearts of false leaders, condemning them for their rebellion, self-will and false doctrine. In their own persistent self-will, they continue toward their own destruction. Whole societies can become corrupt, such as those living at the time of the flood that were destroyed because of their wickedness. The Apostle Paul tells us that the return of Christ to judge the world will be of similar circumstance.

> *Don't let anyone deceive you in any way, for that day* (Christ's return) *will not come until the rebellion occurs and the man of lawlessness is revealed, the man doomed to destruction. He will oppose and will exalt himself over everything that is called God or is worshiped, so that he sets himself up in God's temple, proclaiming himself to be God"* (2 Thessalonians 2:3-4).

People must not be misled in their thinking or by false doctrine, which is doctrine of demons. *"The Spirit clearly says that in later times some will abandon the faith and follow deceiving spirits and things taught by demons. Such teachings come through hypocritical liars, whose consciences have been seared as with a hot iron"* (1 Timothy 4:1-2). When people know the Scriptures, they can say, *"we will no longer be infants, tossed back and forth by the waves, and blown here and there by every wind of teaching and by the cunning and craftiness of men in their deceitful scheming"* (Eph 4:14).

The very sad observation is that far more people are doing 'their own thing' and calling themselves religious than there are people who call themselves 'Christians' and are doing the 'right thing.' For your own good, do not 'go the way of Cain'.

Chapter 5

~ Attitude ~

Have you ever met someone who always wanted to control things? Are you like that?

It seems that we spend a lot of time trying to keep things under control. We may try to keep the budget under control, only to have something happen, like when my freezer up and died of old age. There went my budget. We try to keep our children under control; we want to keep our weight under control. We try to control so many things that our days can be filled with that effort. I know I spend a lot of time in this area.

Some time ago, I came to the conclusion that I had a little control over a few things, absolutely no control over most things, and ***total*** control over only one thing. How many things can you totally control? I would find it interesting to know what you think you can control.

My oldest sister and I were driving one day and, as usual, began a serious discussion. We started to talk about attitudes. She immediately began to mention people and situations that caused her to have a bad attitude. My reply was that people and situations should not cause her to have a bad attitude. She quickly challenged that statement and gave me some examples of people and situations that could immediately change her attitude. Her heated response reminded me of a bumper sticker I had once seen. ***"Caution, I can go from Angel to Bitch in 2.6 seconds."*** I am not saying that the bumper sticker was applying to my sister, but I realized my comment was probably changing her attitude at that very moment. Did that mean I had control over her attitude?

It is true that people and situations often do seem to change our attitude, sometimes not for the better. But this should not be the case. If people and situations could, indeed, ***control*** my attitude, I would be in very serious trouble. Furthermore, if people and situations can even ***affect*** my attitude, I would be in serious trouble. I can understand when people protest, "But people and situations do affect my attitude". And maybe they do, at least for a few minutes, but not for any length of time. Initial reactions are understandable. But if we continue in that attitude for any length of time, we will be guilty of ***giving*** someone else ***control*** of our attitude, which might make us end up unhappy, lacking joy and peace in our lives. We need to know that we can be firmly in charge of our own attitudes.

It is true, and too often the case, that we let people and situations affect and, sometimes, keep control of our attitude. This is sadly the case when some people think poorly of us, resulting in our own attitudes about ourselves being lowered. Then we suffer. But, with a moment's reflection, we will realize that this need not be the case and, in fact, should not be the case. I can let people and situations cause an attitude change in me, but I can also keep my "cool", if I choose. I do not have to let people get my "goat" (read attitude), if that is not my wish. When I think about it, I know no one can change my attitude but me. If I let people change my attitude, it is because I let them, not because they have the power or capability to change my attitude over my own determination. This is true for all situations. I am impressed with my current pastor, because when he encounters adverse situations while working on cars, he always keeps a positive attitude, even if he has to return at a later date to work on the problem.

The truth is that I have control over, and total responsibility for, my attitude. I understand that there are many things that can affect my attitude, ***if*** I choose to let them, but when I stand before God, I am the only one who will be held accountable for the attitude that I keep. Something may cause me to become angry or irritated, but it is totally up to me as to what I shall do about it. No one can keep me angry, unless I want to stay angry. No one can keep my feelings hurt, unless I want to stay that way. I may try to blame someone for my attitude, but my attitude is my responsibility alone.

The Apostle Paul addresses this very thing.

> *For it is not those who hear the law who are righteous in God's sight, but it is those who obey the law who will be declared righteous. (Indeed, when Gentiles, who do not have the law, do by nature things required by the law, they are a law for themselves, even though they do not have the law, since they show that the requirements of the law are written on their hearts, their consciences also bearing witness, and their thoughts now accusing, now even defending them.) This will take place on the day when God will judge men's secrets through Jesus Christ, as my gospel declares.* (Romans 2: 13-16)

God goes to the heart of the situation. If you think about it, you will realize that your actions are the result of your thoughts. You decide to do something and then you do it. You may say to me, "But something will happen and before I even think about it, I get mad and start yelling." My answer concerning that is, "No, this is probably not the first time this has happened to you; you have done that before, and you have decided that that reaction and response is okay for you." Your previous thoughts accepted as 'okay' an immediate response of getting mad and yelling. You could have decided earlier that you were going to keep your 'cool' and respond in the right manner to adverse situations. I admit this will take mental determination (read attitude) and possibility a lot of practice. There is no use to beat yourself up when you react badly—just use the experience as a determination to control your attitude next time. You ***can*** change your behavior (read reaction). In fact, God ***requires*** you to change your thoughts and attitudes, which will result in a change of behavior (read actions).

It is to your benefit that God judges thoughts and intentions as well as actions. Consider this: when you intend to do a good deed for someone, but it does not work out the way you intended, before God, who judges the thoughts and attitudes, you get credit for what you intended, not for what happened—unless it was your fault. It works the other way, too. Do not forget what Jesus said about committing adultery—it can be done in the heart—you may not get to the bed part, but you are still guilty of adultery in God's eyes. It is very important that we control our thoughts. I may decide to rob a bank. I may get a gun, put it in my coat pocket, and start walking toward the bank. Let us say that as I start to cross the street, I get run over and killed by a big truck. I may never physically rob the bank, but before God, who judges my thought and attitudes, I am guilty of robbing a bank. God knows all of our thoughts.

> *O Lord, you have searched me and you know me. You know when I sit and when I rise; you perceive my thoughts from afar. You discern my going out and my lying down; you are familiar with all my ways. Before a word is on my tongue you know it completely, O Lord. Search me, O God, and know my heart; test me and know my anxious thoughts. See if there is any offensive way in me, and lead me in the way everlasting.* (Psalm 139: 1-4; 23-24)

I would not want a God who could not do this with me. I would not want a God from whom I could keep secrets or hide things. If I could hide my thoughts from God, I would probably spend a lot of time trying to do that very thing. A lot of people would like to have a God from whom they could hide thoughts. For those people, I have some very bad news.

Since God does know my thoughts, he knows I can control my attitude. In the Bible, we have a lesson on the importance of the way we control our attitude.

> *For the word of God is living and active. Sharper than any double-edged sword, it penetrates even to dividing soul and spirit, joints and marrow; it judges the thoughts and attitudes of the heart. Nothing in all creation is hidden from God's sight. Everything is uncovered and laid bare before the eyes of him to whom we must give account.* (Hebrews 4: 12-13)

When the Bible says that God is going to judge something, it is a wise thing to see what it is that will be judged, and how we are going to be responsible. It is good to know that we ourselves can control our thoughts and attitudes, not someone else.

As Jesus Christ, the living and active word of God (John 1: 1-5, 14), judges our thoughts and attitudes, he will divide the soul and spirit. It will be like a real sword cutting the body apart at the joints and cutting through a bone to reveal what is inside. We are not able to do these things ourselves, but our Savior and Lord is able, and does, and will do so during the judgment. We may not have considered that there is any difference between our thought and attitudes, but the Bible tells us that there is.

If we put Hebrews 4: 12 into block form, we see this more clearly.

Column 1	Column 2
Soul	Spirit
Joints (body)	Marrow (body)
Thoughts (mind)	Attitudes (spirit)

Our soul is to be compared with joints for the body and thoughts of the heart (mind). Our spirit is to be compared with bone marrow for the body and controls our attitude.

Consider the purpose of the joints of a body. The joints of the body allow for movement and animation. Without the joints, we would not be able to work, to move about, or to put into action the thoughts that we have. It is because we have joints in our body that we can live and express ourselves. Some people could not talk if they could not move their hands. Without joints for the body, we could not even give someone a loving hug or embrace.

The bone marrow is that white fatty tissue inside the bone that develops red and white blood cells (among other things). If the marrow of the body is unhealthy and red and white blood cells are not developed, then the body will be weak and sickly, and if the condition continues, it can easily result in physical death. The marrow is to be equated with my attitude. If my attitude is unhealthy, my spiritual life will be weak and sickly, and if nothing is done, eternal spiritual death will result. It is my attitude that determines my spiritual health. The attitude that is so important is my attitude toward the God of Heaven. It is my spirit that controls my attitude. A person's spirit is to be in charge of that person's soul. This is to say that our attitude will control our thoughts. A good attitude = good thoughts. A bad attitude = bad thoughts.

God will judge first the attitude of my spirit. The Bible even instructs us what our attitude should be. Philippians 2:5 states: *"Your attitude should be the same as that of Christ Jesus:"*

The scripture then goes on in the following verses to explain what Christ's attitude was when he lived on earth, which is exactly what it was before he came to earth. Christ's attitude was the same in the eternal past, when he was on earth, and now as he is glorified in heaven. My attitude should be exactly the same as his. I am responsible to make sure that my attitude ***is*** the same attitude as that of Christ Jesus. By his grace he will help us even in this, but it is our responsibility to have this attitude, because we will be judged according to our attitude.

Let us find out what Christ's attitude was, so that we can make our attitude the same. If you do not make your attitude the same as Christ Jesus', then you will just be a hearer of the Word and not a doer of the Word, and you will not be righteous before God. (Romans 2: 13). I must caution at this time not to think that salvation, justification, and eternal life are the results of actions (works) on our part. *"For it is by grace you have been saved, through faith—and this not from yourselves, it is the gift of God—not by works, so that no one can boast"* (Eph 2:8-9). Here I am simply talking about righteous actions in obedience to the Will of God ***after*** I am saved.

Philippians 2:5-8 describes for us what Christ's attitude was when in human form. *"Your attitude should be the same as that of Christ Jesus: Who, being in very nature God, did not consider equality with God something to be grasped, but made himself nothing, taking the very nature of a servant, being made in human likeness. And being found in appearance as a man, he humbled himself and became obedient to death—even death on a cross!"*

So what was Christ's attitude? Christ's attitude was that of being totally submissive (read totally obedient) to the Father's will, to make himself nothing in that submissiveness, to humble himself, and become obedient even at the price of death on a cross! This attitude must be our own. If we are to be spiritually healthy and not sickly, we must have an attitude of submissiveness (obedience) before God, humble ourselves to nothing of our own, and become obedient to whatever God has planned for each of us.

You may say you cannot do this by yourself, and I agree. It is impossible for us to do on our own, but at this point, we are not talking about actions—we are only talking about our attitude. Of course, you are going to need help in doing God's will. The Apostle John tells us Christ's words on this matter. *"I am the vine; you are the branches. If a man remains* (abides) *in me and I in him, he will bear much fruit; apart from me you can do nothing"* (John 15:5). We must start with the right attitude! The Beatitudes (Matthew 5:2-11) are helpful in describing this attitude.

If our attitude is the correct one, then our thoughts, which result from our attitude, will be sound as well. If I have the wrong attitude, I will have bad thoughts. If I have the right attitude, I will have good thoughts.

It is from our thoughts that our soul works through the body our acts of obedience and mercy and love. A dear friend of mine would say, "Jesus with skin on."

Since the only thing that I have total control over is my attitude, it seems wise that I make sure that my attitude is the correct attitude. It is the only thing that I will be ***totally*** responsible for, and for which I will be judged.

You are correct if you tell me that your works will be judged as well, but you must also agree that the quality of your works is dependent upon your attitude. A bad attitude—bad quality of works. A good attitude—then a good quality of works.

It will not be good for me if I allow my attitude to include hate, envy, jealously, discord, strife, vanity, selfish ambition, or the like. *"If you keep on biting and devouring each other, watch out or you will be destroyed by each other"* (Galatians 5:15; Galatians 5:19). I sometimes have to spend a lot of time correcting my attitude to that of a servant of God. God has been gracious to us in giving the Holy Spirit to dwell in us in order to help us, to work in us both to will and to do His good Pleasure. *"For it is God who works in you to will and to act according to his good purpose"* (Philippians 2:13).

A quick example for us, which has been so hard for many, but which Christ Jesus so lovingly demonstrated toward us when he forgives us of our sins against him and the Father is: *"For if you forgive men when they sin against you, your heavenly Father will also forgive you. But if you do not forgive men their sins, your Father will not forgive your sins."* (Matthew 6:14-15). What is your attitude toward this? Are there some people that you 'just cannot forgive'? Look again at the verse. It is not just a nice suggestion for you to take or leave, but it is an attitude of Christ concerning forgiveness for you as you forgive others. You had better get let control of your attitude about forgiveness. Is there anyone on your list that you have not forgiven? When you stand before Christ (your judge) and your eternal future is dependent on how you forgave others—do not be caught with a defective attitude of past unforgiveness.

So, how's your attitude (read obedience to God)? How are you handling the only thing over which you have total control? Are you keeping your thoughts under control? We are told in 2 Corinthians 10:5-6 this very thing: *"We demolish arguments and every pretension that sets itself up against the knowledge of God, and we take captive every thought to make it obedient to Christ."* Consciously take control of your attitude!

Chapter 7

~ Salvation & Other Things ~

In the matter of salvation, the Apostle Peter tells us that God goes to great lengths in order to save people. *"The Lord is not slow in keeping his promise, as some understand slowness. He is patient with you, not wanting anyone to perish, but everyone to come to repentance"* (2 Peter 3:9).

This is true from the very beginning and is true today. God was very patient with Cain (Genesis 4) in his effort to bring Cain from his own willful disobedience (read sin) to salvation. But Cain would have no part of God's patient effort, so we have the third person to be on this earth refusing God's will and purpose—and going his own way! Think of it—the very first child to be born on this earth to Adam and Eve, rebelling against God, refusing to humble himself and to do the 'right' thing, which would bring blessings. Cain refused to acknowledge God in the way that God, as Creator, and, even at this point, as Redeemer from satanic influence and destruction, wanted to be acknowledged! God had every right as 'Creator' and 'Redeemer' to expect proper acknowledgment. And yes, he has every right to expect the same from us today! But Cain, in his own willful sinfulness, chose instead to be separated from God, so that he could do his 'religious worship' (to have his own religious expression) his own way. Cain did not receive salvation and eternal life from God, even though God patiently tried to save Cain. All the 'religions' of the world that refuse the worship of God through Jesus Christ have 'gone the way of

Cain' (Jude 11) and have willingly separated themselves from God—even as Cain did.

What we need to understand is that God loves us, is patient with us and does all he can to bring us to salvation. We read in John 3:16, *"For God so loved the world that he gave his one and only Son, that whoever believes in him shall not perish but have eternal life."* At the same time, we need to understand that God will not save us against our own will—he will let us do our own thing! God let Cain go his own way, and as Cain did so, he probably influenced many to do the same thing. It is hard to know how much influence Cain had on the society of his day, but it is clear that mankind's rebellion against God caused them to be destroyed in the flood. All but eight people perished in that deluge of water. This should caution us that *"Whoever believes in the Son has eternal life, but whoever rejects the Son will not see life, for God's wrath remains on him"* (John 3:36).

As I stated in an earlier chapter (Chapter 2) the majority of people of this world will not be saved but will perish—because of their own self will.

~ *The Elect* ~

God is infinite in his characteristics and attributes. Among these are his wisdom, understanding, and purpose. We are finite and, consequently, though we can understand what is said, we are at a loss to comprehend the 'why'(the wisdom and purpose). This is true concerning 'why' God, in his own sovereignty, chooses who will be saved and calls them the 'elect'. We know what the Scripture says, but we are not able to wrap our minds around what is said. Proverbs 25:2 says, *"It is the glory of God to conceal a matter; to search out a matter is the glory of kings."* However limited we are, we should still make the attempt to learn as much of God's purpose as He wishes us to learn. Scripture encourages us to do so.

> *If any of you lacks wisdom, he should ask God, who gives generously to all without finding fault, and it will be given to him. But when he asks, he must believe and not doubt, because he who doubts is like a wave of the sea, blown and tossed by the wind. That man should not think he will receive anything from the Lord; he is a double-minded man, unstable in all he does.* (James 1:5-8)

I am not a double-minded man, so, hopefully, I am closer to the glory of a king, because I love to search out a matter. I have asked God for wisdom and have graciously received wisdom from him (I always want more). I have doubted things—not the grace or ability of God—but that what I was doing was the right thing. Recent reflection, because I have taken time to reflect, has encouraged me to keep reflecting about what I do. I do not like painful things, so I have determined not to go against what God has decreed—as well as to do the things God does decree. Age is no buffer to pain, or sorrow, or the necessity to mature spiritually. Going against what God decrees will always be painful for people—now or later or both. Even the 'elect' suffer as they mature spiritually. Like Job, some things that God allows in our lives do not make sense to us—at least at the time. We may never find out about some things until we get to heaven and maybe then we will not even care. But I trust him with all my heart (finally, I might add).

Obedience to God will bring comfort, joy and gladness, and sweet fellowship with God and those who are like-minded. It is the 'elect' who will learn obedience to God and enjoy sweet fellowship with him as they grow.

Although I am not going to take the time in this chapter to establish just how involved God is in everyone's life, even the unbeliever, I do want you to consider two things of God that demonstrate his involvement 24/7. First, there is not a sinner in the world, among more than six billion people, that when he whispers for forgiveness of sin—but that God hears immediately and responds—immediately— with grace, mercy and forgiveness. Yes, it is even God who draws the sinner to himself. God draws the 'elect' to himself. And the 'elect' comes to God.

Second, there is not an atom in the universe whose many positive charges in the nucleus is not continuously held together by Christ. (Col 1:17). Not one atom, or proton, or electron, in the universe, is outside Christ's continuous attention. Scientists do not understand what holds all the positive nuclear proton charges together and just call it the 'strong force', but it is the continuous power of Christ who is the eternal 'strong force.' When Christ releases his hold on all the atoms of the universe, we will behold the words of Peter (2 Peter 3:10) when he says, *"But the day of the Lord will come like a thief. The heavens will disappear with a* ***roar****; the* ***elements*** *will be destroyed by fire, and the earth and everything in it will be laid bare."* (Emphasis mine.) The word 'roar' is the Greek 'oruomai', which was as loud, in Peter's time, as anything could be. At that time, thunder was probably the loudest noise heard. We would know it today as a nuclear explosion—where the whole universe explodes in a giant nuclear fireball. That is going to be LOUD!! All the elements in the universe are made up of atoms, and the moment that Christ releases his hold upon them, they will erupt into a giant nuclear conflagration the likes of which we cannot even imagine. Everything that exists in the physical world is potential nuclear fire. Just think: we eat potential fire (food is made with elements—atoms), we drink potential fire (atoms in water), we wear potential fire, we drive potential fire, in fact we are potential fire—and when Christ releases his hold on atoms, everything will disappear in a roar and be destroyed by fire. Thankfully, we will have spiritual bodies at that time, which are not made up of atoms.☺ The flood destroyed a lot of things the first time, fire will destroy the second time, and now you know how it will be done!! The 'elect' will not be destroyed—they will live forever. Oh, Yes! Hell is forever also!

My point is: God is intricately involved in our lives for his eternal purpose. This includes everyone. *"There came a man* (John the Baptist) *who was sent from God; his name was John. He came as a witness to testify concerning that light* (Christ Jesus), *so that through him all* (all) *men might believe. He himself was not the light; he came only as a witness to the light. The true light that gives light to every* (every) *man* (person) *was coming into the world"* (John 1: 6-9).

The real question is: 'Do you want to be one of the 'elect'?' Do you want to be among those whom God will 'save' and 'sanctify'? If you do—then you must respond to the 'light' (spiritual illumination) when it shines on you!!

God's purpose is to redeem the 'elect' and to judge the ungodly. God will redeem the 'elect' who had been lost to sin and death through Adam; to give his 'elect' eternal life and joy in his presence; to sanctify them—to make them holy, even as he is holy; and to prepare them for life with himself for eternity. This, of course, is not a natural human desire—even for Christians, until the Holy Spirit comes to dwell and work within us (Philippians 2:13) and God's light (spiritual illumination) shines on us.

To end this, consider (wrap your mind around this): God has total sovereignty and authority concerning salvation, and, at the same time, man (we) has total responsibility in his salvation, in that we must respond to God in obedience and faith. Can our finite minds understand this?

~ Final Thought ~

Our 'spiritual desire' is to please God, but also within us are the desires of the sinful world and a personal sin nature (Romans 7:14-25;

Gal 5:19-21b). God in his sovereignty and purpose gives his 'elect' a 'faith' of which Christ is the author and perfecter (Heb 12:2), so our faith is a supernatural faith which will never fail, even though we may, and will, stumble at times. This faith, which is given to the elect, leads the elect to believe in and accept Christ for salvation (Ephesians 2:8-9). Because of God's sovereignty, this supernatural faith, because it is from Christ, is only given to the elect. It takes understanding to apply this to John 3:16.

Salvation ~ Phase One ~ From the Penalty of Sin

Our salvation is three-fold. First, our salvation is from the penalty of sin, which is eternal separation from God, which we call spiritual death. Second, our salvation is from the power of sin over us. Scripture calls this part of our salvation sanctification, and it takes up all the time from our becoming a Christian until we die physically. And third, our salvation is from the presence of sin. We experience this part when we physically die and go to heaven, where sin will not be allowed to enter. Satan is presently allowed to enter heaven (Job 1:6; Rev 12:10), but that will not continue for much longer.

Accepting Christ as our Savior and Redeemer and Lord is the first part of our salvation. It saves us from the penalty of sin. The Scripture calls this being 'born again.' That is exactly what happens. We are made totally new creations in Christ—spiritually. We become spiritual children of God—who takes the responsibility of being our Heavenly Father. Our position before God is now that of being his spiritual children perfected in Christ with Christ's eternal life and our being given his perfect righteousness.

While the above is our *spiritual position* before God, it is *not yet* our physical or experiential position, because our *physical experience* is that we still have a physical body, with a sin nature, and we are still alive on earth. Both positions are true. Eventually, when we die physically, our spiritual position and our physical experience will be the same. I hope you have understood what I have said, because it is vital to our understanding of our present circumstance as a Christian. We have been 'made perfect' in Christ, but we are not yet with him in heaven. While we are still on earth, our salvation is not yet complete—that is to say, we are not yet saved from the attacks or the presence of sin. Our second and third phase of salvation is not yet complete. It is during the second phase of our salvation, our sanctification or the process of learning to struggle with sin and to overcome sin (spiritual victory) that we face 'hell on earth' in our fight with Satan and our own sin nature. (Ephesians 6:10-18).

2 Corinthians 5:17describes what it means to be a new creation. *"Therefore, if anyone is in Christ, he (she) is a* ***new creation****; the old has gone, the new has come!"* (Emphasis mine.) Read verses 18-21 as well. I do not want to belabor a point, but I would like to share with you what I shared in a recent Bible study, which should be helpful. I put things in table form, and while it does not exhaust the old things or list all the new—you will get the idea.

Old/gone	New/come
Only prayer guaranteed to be heard—prayer of confession. Hostile to God. Romans 8:7.	Total access to God through grace. Romans 5:2. Peace with God. Romans 5:1.
Spiritual & physical death. Romans 3:10; 20; 23.	Gift of Eternal life. John 3:16; 10:28; Romans 6:23; 1John 2:25.
Under the Law. Rom 6:14.	Under Grace. Rom 6:14.
Living under the Law of sin and death. Rom 8:3.	Living under the Law of the Spirit of Life. Rom 8:2.
Condemned to Hell. Rom 8:1.	No Condemnation. Rom 8:1 (This does not mean that we do not sin.)*
Not in Christ. Rom 8:1. Living according to the sin nature. Rom 8:5.	"In Christ." Rom 8:1; Rom 6:3-4. Living according to the Spirit. Rom 5:b.**
Have no heavenly inheritance. Rom 8:17.	Have an eternal inheritance. Rom 8:17.
Do not suffer for Christ. Rom 8:17. Will not be glorified. Rom 8:30.	Suffer for Christ. Rom 8:17; Matthew 5:10-11. Are glorified with Christ. Rom 8:30.

Do not have God's love, peace, Gal 5:19.	Have God's love, peace, & joy or joy. Gal 5:22.
Not a child of God. Rom 8:16.	A child (adopted) of God. Rom 8:16.
Do not have the promise that God will work all things for good. Rom 8:28.	Do have the promise that God will work all things together for good. Rom 8:28.***
Will get the wages of all sins committed—punishment. Rev 20:15.	Will be rewarded for all the good works done in Christ. Eph 2:10; 1 Cor. 3:8-14.
Do not have the Spirit's help. Rom 8:26; 1 Cor 10:12-13.	Do have the Spirit's indwelling help. Rom 8:26; I Cor 10:12-13.
Normal (human) faith, which will fail in trials and temptations. Matthew 13:21-22.	Supernatural faith, which comes from Christ, which will not fail, even under the harshest testing and trials. Heb 12:2.
Not a victorious conqueror. Rom 8:37.	A victorious conqueror. Rom 8:37.

* Christians sin but not as a continuing thing or as a lifestyle. Because Christians are under grace (no longer under the Law), they are never condemned (Romans 8:1). They may well suffer temporary consequences of their sin (which I have) in this temporary life, but Christians will not suffer the eternal penalty of sin. I am saying that there is a difference between the temporary consequence of sin, for a Christian, and the eternal penalty for sin, for the unbeliever. It is the Law that condemns us, but we are no longer under the law, but under grace (Romans 6:14). Grace does not condemn us—even though we sin at times. God will convict us to repent and to maintain fellowship with him, but he does not condemn us.

** Christians should be led by the Spirit. This means that we need to listen and hear the small voice within us when God speaks. There are times that I have heard his voice but was not obedient to it. This was not good for me, in fact, was to my own hurt, though not a permanent hurt. It is even these things that God promises to use for my own good. When God speaks, we may hear it easily, but sometimes he speaks so softly we must pay close attention. Sometimes it is Satan's voice or that of a demon—so we must check what is said to us with consistency with the Scripture. Every time it is about doubting God's Word, or for our vanity, or conceit, etc, you can be sure it is Satan speaking.

*** Romans 8:28 is an awesome promise to the Christian. To 'love' God is to be obedient to him. (John 14: 15, 21, 23). God promises to work "all" things for the Christian's good. Temporary consequences that we suffer end up working for our good. The good is in this life, as well as in molding our eternal character for the next life. This promise is retroactive for all things that have happened in our lives, even those things that happened before we gave our life to Christ. If you can not wrap your faith around this, then, one: you do not understand the eternal power and love of God, and/or, two: your faith is human and not authored by Christ. (Hebrews 12:2).

The above table does not exhaust all that 2 Cor 5:17 includes, but you get a beginning as to what it includes. I am glad to be "born again" into the family of God. I am grateful that God desires to be 'My Heavenly Father' and takes upon himself all that a Heavenly Father is responsible for to his children.

When we have accepted what Christ did for us on the Cross and invite Christ into our life to be our Lord and Savior—phase one of our salvation is completed. At this point, the blood of Christ has cleansed us from all our sins (past, present, and future), and our ***position*** before God the Father is that of a new creation, and we are as pure and righteous before him (Our Heavenly Father) as is Christ himself. We are then placed under God's grace—never to be condemned for sin again. (Romans 6:14; 8:1). If our conscience still bothers us, all we need to do is ask God who will cleanse our conscience for us as stated in Hebrews 10:22. This is our ***eternal spiritual position*** before God because of being baptized into Christ (Romans 6:3-4). We are identified, by baptism, with the death, burial, and resurrection of Christ before the Father. Our ***personal physical experience*** is different, unfortunately, because we have not yet actually died physically (as Christ did), and we are still subject to sin and temptation, in the body, which is the subject of the second phase of our salvation—that is our sanctification.

~ Salvation, Phase Two – Sanctification ~

Sanctification is God's way of working in our lives here on earth to make our personal experience be as close as possible to what our eternal spiritual position before Him will be when we are in heaven. We are instructed by God, through Paul, to consider ourselves dead to sin but alive to God through Christ (Romans 6:8-13). So at this point, there is a difference between our spiritual position before God and our physical experience of still being alive on earth. When we die physically, our spiritual position and our physical experience will be the same. God deals with us as if we are already dead, buried, and resurrected, though we have not yet died. This is why Paul says, *"I have been crucified with Christ and I no longer live, but Christ lives in me. The life I live in the body, I live by faith* (supernatural faith that does not fail) *in the Son of God, who loved me and gave himself for me. I do not set aside the grace of God, for if righteousness could be gained through the law, Christ died for nothing"* (Gal 2:20-22).

Paul is saying that by baptism he died with Christ, was buried with Christ, and was resurrected with Christ. That the life he lives in the body now—he lives by faith in the Son of God, who loved him and gave himself for Paul. Since Paul is now dead, his spiritual position and his physical experience are both the same. J.B. Phillips, in his translation of the Bible, says to 'pretend' that you are dead to sin but alive to God in Christ. This is to say that your physical experience is not the same as your spiritual position before God, but we are to live physically as if it were the same. This is to understand not to let sin overcome you while in the flesh. We are to let our 'spirit' say 'no' to doing things that we know are 'sin'.

Stage one of salvation is painless for us. It was Christ who suffered, and bled, and died—on the cross. It was painful for Christ, who died in our place, who suffered death for us. We can correctly say that we did not choose to be a sinner with a sin nature, which is true. God can rightfully say that he paid the price to set us free from the penalty of sin, because he suffered for us—in our place.

If it is painful for Christ to discipline and work in our lives for our sanctification in overcoming the power of sin in our lives, then he suffers with us in this part of our salvation, too. This part of our salvation does not need to be painful for us, but it generally is—at least at times. It is in this part of our salvation that we kick and scream, cry and weep, have pity parties, suffer and bleed, moan and groan, and generally feel sorry for ourselves. It does not have to be like this; it just depends on how much sin has gotten a hold on us and how much we resist the firm determination of God to remove the power of sin in our lives. God is gracious and at times completely removes the desire for a particular sinful habit. We may know of people who have been blest in this way. For some of us, the removal of sin's desire and addiction can be very stressful. It will be different for everyone, but God is determined to sanctify (remove the power of sin from) all of his children.

It is a good question to ask why God wants us to go through the sanctification process, which generally causes us to suffer. I have asked that question. The best that I have answered is that it is through this process he makes our present experience more like our spiritual position before Him. It is during this process that he builds our character, teaches us submission and obedience, develops the fruit of the Spirit in us to love and serve others and to learn to forgive others, and generally prepares us to rule and reign with him in eternity. If that is not enough of an answer, then try this—because it is his will!

Phase one of salvation is absolutely the same for everyone: a man, a woman, a child, or a young person, and that involves faith in what Christ did for us on the Cross. It is in phase two of salvation that the process of sanctification varies from person to person, between men and women and children. Each of us has our own particular life situations, wherein we must struggle with sin's temptations, withstanding each trial with the help of the Holy Spirit. We are lead by the Spirit to become more like Jesus in our love and service to others, no matter what form that service may take.

Unfortunately, in much of today's world, we do not receive the spiritual training we need, as conventional religion and our world culture is not focused on Christ. Take marriage as an example. God uses marriage to sanctify both the husband and wife. It is in marriage that each spouse should learn submission—to each other as well as to God—and to learn that love is a commitment—not a fuzzy warm feeling that will not be there all the time. God has established marriage as a unique union between husband and wife to help each other guard against temptation. But today's society has put aside this provision of God in favor of all types of living arrangements, based on the sin nature's desires. God's rules are there for a purpose and are neglected only at our hurt—which also hurts our children, our extended families, our society, etc. As mentioned before the sanctification process lasts from the time we become a Christian until we are taken home to be with Christ. Each sanctification process is tailor designed by God for each individual—since no two of us are exactly alike. However, the final goal in all sanctification efforts is designed for the same results—to make us all more like our Lord and Savior.

~ Salvation – The Final Phase ~

The final phase of our salvation occurs the moment that we die physically. It is at that moment that we are totally perfected in the presence of God, which is to say that our 'physical position' before God becomes exactly the same as our 'spiritual position' became at the moment of our salvation. We will be 'free' from the presence of sin forever and will enjoy the presence of God in heaven for the same amount of time. We will reap the reward of our salvation, which will include an inheritance with Christ (Romans 8:17); it will include an eternal reward for faithful and obedient service to Christ as Lord (1 Corinthians 3:10-17), and it will include a new eternal body and life eternal. Amen? Amen!!

Chapter 8

~ Baptism ~

There is much confusion among Christians, let alone everyone else, as to what we should understand about Christian baptism. This chapter should help you to understand the Scriptural explanation of baptism and an introduction to the work and ministry of the Holy Spirit in this age of grace.

~ Baptism Defined ~

The word baptism comes from the Greek 'baptisis' meaning to dip or immerse, such as when dipping cloth into a dye. The cloth becomes the same color as the dye and is then identified (identical) with that color. There are many kinds of baptisms by various organizations (not just Christian), and the basic meaning of the word *baptism* is IDENTIFICATION. If you are baptized into an organization of some kind, you are identified with that organization. You would consider yourself 'one' with the organization. When being baptized, you may or may not get wet, depending on what constitutes their baptism ritual. In Scripture, the baptism of the "fathers" into Moses in the cloud and the sea had absolutely nothing to do with their getting wet, but with their 'identification' or 'oneness' with the will of God as declared through His prophet Moses (1 Corinthians 10:1-2). In the day of Noah, the eight who were "saved by water" did not get wet, for it was the unbelievers who were immersed (to die) on that occasion (1 Peter 3:20-21). Their 'saving baptism' was their identification with the will of God as revealed through Noah. Those who are firmly identified with righteousness are seen as "baptized", even though they are not sprinkled or immersed in water. The believing thief on the cross beside the Lord Jesus Christ was baptized (that is 'identified') with Christ, before God the Father, when he placed saving faith in the Savior, calling upon Him (Christ) for remembrance (Luke 23:39-43). Christ, Himself, spoke of His identification with sinners (you and me) on the cross ("cursed is he who is hanged on a tree") as a baptism (Luke 12:50).

~ *Spiritual Baptism* ~

In the spiritual sense, to understand the 'True Baptism' is to understand that it is accomplished by God and not by man. It is to say in plain words that no human baptism, regardless of the mode (sprinkling, pouring, immersion), is able to save in the least. A man can baptize you with water so many times that you could become friendly with the fish, but unless God has already been involved, it will do you no good.

The Apostle Paul says, *"One Lord, one faith, one baptism"* in Ephesians 4:5. In 1 Corinthians 12:13, it is stated, *"For we were all baptized by one Spirit into one body—whether Jews or Greeks* (non-Jews or Gentiles), *slave or free—and we were all given the one Spirit to drink."* Scripturally this is the baptism that counts! It is when the Holy Spirit places us into the body of Christ (the Church, which is the body of Christ of which he is the 'Head'). In this spiritual act (not a physical act), we are 'identified' with Christ by being placed into his body, which is the spiritual church. As you can see, this has nothing to do with water, but rather the work of the Holy Spirit placing us into Christ. The Holy Spirit will place us into Christ the moment we accept Christ as our Savior from our sins. It is also at this moment that the Holy Spirit comes into the believer to permanently dwell and empower the believer to live the Christian life. This is indicated by the words, *"And we were all given the one Spirit to drink."* This means that the Holy Spirit comes into us to dwell—eternally!

~ *Grace VS Law* ~

The Holy Spirit will never leave us in this age of grace—as he left those in the Old Testament covenant of being under the law. Christians, those who place their faith and trust in the saving work of Christ on the cross, are taken out from under the condemning finger-pointing of the 'law' (given through Moses), which condemns us to die (because we break the law, i.e. sin), and are placed under the saving grace of Christ, which frees us from the eternal penalty of our sin, which is death or separation from our Loving Heavenly Father. We must be totally righteous to come before the God of Heaven. Christ takes away our sin, which he bore for us on the Cross, and gives us his righteousness, so that we can come before our Loving Heavenly Father as righteous. So, as Christians, we have been taken out from under the condemnation of the law and have been placed under God's loving grace. This does not mean that we do not sin anymore, but it means that if we do sin, we need to recognize it as sin and confess it (1 John 1:8-9). God will be 'faithful' and 'just' to forgive us our sin and to cleanse us from our unrighteousness. God is faithful in forgiving us, because he loves us. God's justice is fulfilled, because Christ has paid the penalty of our sin for us. If we paid the penalty for our own sin, it would cost us death in Hell forever. Because of this grace—and we will forever be in Christ's grace—we will always have the indwelling Holy Spirit, which means we will always have eternal life. Christ promises us that he will never leave us. *"Never will I leave you; never will I forsake you"* (Hebrews 13:5b). Eternal Life is God's gift to us—we had no power to 'get it' on our own, and we do not have the power to 'give it' away (lose it). This is contrary to some men's thinking, those who think a man can give his eternal life away. We do not have the power or the authority, scripturally, to take eternal life from anyone, including ourselves. We should also understand who we are dealing with; God, who gives us eternal life, will not take it from us, because he does not say later, "Oops, I made a mistake!" God does not make mistakes and his gifts and his call to salvation are irrevocable. *"God's gifts and his call are irrevocable"* (Romans 11:29). If you could possibly lose your eternal life as a Christian—and you truly believed that—then you would have to live in constant fear that such a thing might happen. Perfect love casts out such fear.

A New Creation~

I want to make an additional comment concerning eternal security. In 2 Corinthians 5:17 it states, *"Therefore, if anyone is in Christ (placed there by the Holy Spirit), he is a new creation; the old has gone, the new has come!"* If you have been baptized into Christ, you are a new creation! You are not the same old sinner with a 'separate thing' called 'eternal life' stuck in your pocket to do with as you please—you are a totally new creation, in Christ, and a partaker of the divine nature (2 Peter 1:4), and you will be that new creation eternally, never to be changed again or separated from Christ! You are secure.

Being under grace is not a license to sin! God disciplines those whom he loves (Hebrews 12:5-12). God lets us pay a temporary cost for our sin, which is generally very painful, and, thus, He is well able to get our attention. It is my purpose to behave (read—be obedient), so that I do not have to suffer, even temporarily, because of my rebellion and sinfulness. The consequences, though painful, are for our good, because God uses them as a learning process for character building—to perfect us—into being like Christ. If you do not want to be like Christ, your only other option is to be like the Devil and to suffer the consequence of sin—eternally. Do not forget that there is no water in Hell, like the living water that exists in Heaven, and Hell is a very thirsty place.

~ Emotions? ~

The Baptism of the Spirit concerns the absolute and total union with Christ and his Church. It has nothing to do with any particular emotional experience. It is the act of the Spirit as he places the believer into Christ. This is accomplished in the Spiritual realm. It is true that when the load of sin is removed from our soul and spirit, generally, there will be an emotional experience of forgiveness and cleansing and of our being released from our guilt of sin. Often, great joy and gladness will accompany that experience—due to God's forgiveness and God's love and joy filling our hearts. The Baptism of the Spirit itself is not even felt. There are Christians who can not put a 'date' or 'time' to their decision of accepting Christ as their Lord and Savior. They know that they have done it, but their attitude of submission and acceptance of Christ extended over a period of time, and they do not have a specific 'date' to share. This is not a problem. If people want a 'date', they can take any 'date' and affirm (reaffirm) their faith in Christ. If it is not a problem to the person involved and they know that they are 'in Christ', then it is totally inappropriate to demand that they 'get a date'. If you can observe the 'fruit of the Spirit' in their lives, they do not need a 'date'. If you can not observe the 'fruit of the Spirit' in their lives, they still do not need a date—they need salvation itself.

It is the Holy Spirit himself who testifies that we are children of God, and the Holy Spirit is fully capable of informing us when we are not. *"The Spirit himself testifies with our spirit that we are God's children"* (Romans 8:16). It is true that there will be those who will not be able to enter heaven when they think that they should (Matthew 7:21-23) and that they are self-deceived. If they had only checked the Scripture and determined if the 'Jesus' that they served was really the 'Jesus' of the Scriptures, they would not have been self deceived. This includes such people as Jehovah's Witnesses and Mormons. But such people as these are so self-willed that they will not listen to the Spirit; they will write their own scriptures, and they will listen to seducing spirits. We should also guard against the 'easy believeism' of some Evangelicals who would have people simply repeat a simple prayer for salvation, with no conviction of sin or commitment to Christ. It is not hard to tell these kind of 'confessors' from the real thing, because they lack the "fruit of the Spirit" in their lives.

~ *Symbolic Baptism* ~

Symbolic baptism is applied by man through the use of water. Because we do not see what has taken place in the spiritual realm, we perform a ritual known as 'water baptism'. It is through water baptism that a believer declares visually, for all to see, that he identifies himself/herself with a visible fellowship of believers. This is to symbolize the work of the Holy Spirit placing the believer into the 'Church, the Body of Christ'. The ritual proclaims the reality, but does not take its place. We can be saved by the reality without the ritual, but we can never be saved by the ritual apart from the reality. The ritual is by water. The reality is by the Holy Spirit.

~ *Mode of Symbolic Baptism* ~

Typically, we get so involved over the ritual, which we see, that we often do not even understand what had to take place in the spiritual realm first. We concern ourselves as to the mode of our water baptism—sprinkling, pouring, immersion—and often miss the fact that all three are just a ritual that represents only one spiritual reality. One mode of water baptism may visually represent the death, burial, and resurrection of Christ more succinctly, *in our western mind for burial,* than another. If we consider the burial of Christ—the way it actually happened, we might change our idea about the 'mode' of water baptism. When Christ was 'buried' he was not put six feet (less these days) under ground and covered over with dirt as we do in the Western world. He was wrapped up and placed on a rock ledge in a tomb upon which an angel could sit (Mark 16:5). The tomb was a cave cut out of rock. The way that Christ was 'buried' would not begin to suggest water baptism by immersion to the early church! Christ's death was his being 'cut off' from the living through crucifixion, and we are baptized into his death. We were therefore buried with him into death in order that, just as Christ was raised from the dead through the glory of the Father, we too may live a new life. (Romans 6:3-4). If he had not been dead, which he was, (although some foolishly say he was not), he could have breathed the whole time during his 'burial' phase. Since we do not actually 'kill' people during our 'ritual' of baptism, the fact that we do not breath while we are immersed, I find, is of no importance. I fully accept Western baptism can reflect Western burials—no breathing allowed! I have conducted baptisms by immersion myself, so I do not care about the mode of water baptisms as long as everyone understands what we are doing.

The ritual is by water. The reality is by the Holy Spirit. To count the baptism done by man, in or with water, to be superior to the baptism of the Spirit of God is to disregard the Scripture and to slip into sheer blasphemy! Blasphemy is to disregard and count as nothing, or as profane, the Word of God.

~ Speaking in Tongues? ~

It needs to be stated very plainly that the 'Baptism of the Holy Spirit' is not the same thing as "speaking in tongues", as some would have you believe. The 'Baptism of the Holy Spirit' is as I have described to you above. Speaking in tongues was an early 'gift' of service to confirm God's involvement and confirmation to the early Acts of the Apostles, before the Scriptures were put into written form. Speaking in tongues was a 'gift' given by the Holy Spirit—not a baptism performed by the Spirit.

The amazing phenomena which took place on the day of Pentecost was unique in that there were many who spoke in foreign languages who had never before spoken in a foreign tongue. Not only were they able to miraculously speak a foreign language, but also they were heard by a large group present who could understand what they were saying. This incident on the day of Pentecost is very different than the present-day garbled speech of those claiming to be 'speaking in tongues', which are actually non-definable as known languages and which permit varied 'translations', as the so-called 'translators' are said to be 'moved by the spirit.' God's gift to let the Apostles speak in "tongues" at Pentecost and at other times before the New Testament Scriptures were written was to let people know that something new was happening and that God was approving and causing it to happen. Once the Scriptures were written and the 'Church era was established on the foundation of the Apostles', the gift of speaking in tongues historically died out. Speaking in tongues is common in history in many cultic and pagan circles of worship, and it was reintroduced around 1900 by people who wanted more 'spiritual passion or emotion' in their worship. I agree that we need passion in our worship of God, and we are to love him with all our heart and soul (the seat of feelings and emotions), and mind (Matthew 22:37). We are also to worship God in "spirit and in truth" (John 4:23-24), neither of which is necessarily emotional. If you truly want to know how 'spiritual' you are, check the "fruit of the Spirit" (Galatians 5:22-25) produced in you—a list which does not include any of the 'gifts' of the Spirit. The gifts of the Spirit are for service to others, not for worshiping God, other than the fact that you worship God by serving others. The 'speaking in tongues' movement became a gauge as to how spiritual you were, which is totally unscriptural. It became a point of 'pride' to speak in 'tongues' or a necessary thing in order to participate in their fellowship and worship with them, which is also unscriptural and sinful. I repeat: their pride in using tongues to demonstrate spirituality is unscriptural and sinful.

~ Filling of the Spirit? ~

The 'filling' of the Spirit is not the same as the Baptism of the Spirit. A careful study of the Scripture will show that the 'Baptism of the Spirit' is a one-time event (the placing of a person into the body of Christ), while the 'filling of the Spirit' is a continuous and repeatable experience. The filling of the Spirit concerns our yielding to the will of the Spirit and our being strengthened by the Spirit to accomplish God's will in our life.

~ Christ's Baptism ~

While we are addressing water baptism, it should be noted that the Holy Spirit did not baptize Jesus at the time John baptized our Lord with water. The baptism of Jesus by John the 'baptizer' has to do with our Lord's induction into the holy priesthood according to the Mosaic regulations. When a priest was ordained to the priesthood by sprinkling with water, he was also anointed with oil by pouring. Oil poured was a 'symbol' of the anointing by the Spirit of God, which would occur at the same time as the sprinkling with water. The 'symbol' of the anointing of Christ was when the Holy Spirit descended on Christ in the bodily form of a dove. The dove 'symbolized' his anointing with the Oil of Heaven, just as the sprinkled water signified His sanctified humanity prepared for service as our High Priest. Remember that Christ's priesthood was not after the same order as that of the Levites, because Christ was of the tribe of Judah and his priesthood was after the order of Melchizedek. The 'symbols' for the ordaining into the priesthood of Christ would, therefore, be different. It should be noted that while Christ was anointed into his High Priesthood he was not baptized by the Holy Spirit into the body of Christ as we are, because Christ was the body into which we are baptized (identified by being placed into Christ). John's baptism was to signify repentance of sin—Christ did not have to repent of sin, but in order to fulfill all righteousness he did need to be ordained into his High Priesthood role.

~ *The Church* ~

As you should understand at this point, everyone who believes and accepts Christ's sacrifice on the Cross is at that moment 'identified' with the death, burial, and resurrection of Christ through the baptism of the Holy Spirit. It is that work of the Holy Spirit that identifies us with Christ by placing us into Christ, who is the head of the Church, and we become a part of his body. We become fellow members of the body from the first one who was added on the Day of Pentecost until the last one will be added, just before the rapture or removal of that part of the Church which is still on the earth. The body, the Church, is not yet complete, but we are all connected because of Christ.

~ *The New Birth* ~

Our 'new birth' is not to be confused with the Baptism of the Holy Spirit. It happens at the same time, but they are two different events. Our new birth is when we become a new creation in Christ. It is when Christ comes into us (John 14:20). The baptism is when we are placed into Christ. Consider it a directional thing. Christ into us, we are place into Christ. Paul states in Galatians 2:20, *"I have been crucified with Christ and I no longer live, but Christ lives in me. The life I live in the body, I live by faith in the Son of God, who loved me and gave himself for me."* We have an individual relationship with Christ, as well as a unity with all believers.

~ *The Sealing of the Spirit* ~

The 'sealing of the Spirit' is a third thing that happens at the same time as the 'new birth' and the 'Baptism of the Holy Spirit'. You might kiss, and hug, and step on your girlfriend's feet all at the same time, but they are not all the same thing. ☺ Every believer is sealed with the Spirit at the same instant that he is born again, just as he is baptized by the Holy Spirit at the same instant that he is born again. These are all separate things, though they occur at the same time. To be sealed by the Holy Spirit is the stamp of God's ownership, signifying that we are his property (Ephesians 1:13; 4:30; 2 Corinthians 1:22). Demons can easily see this seal of ownership, but they depend on the fact that you are not aware of it, or forget to whom you belong, or just who you really are, and they will do everything to give you 'hell', while they are able to do so.

~ *The Indwelling Spirit* ~

The Scripture is very clear in its teaching that all believers, during the Church age, are indwelt by the Holy Spirit (1 Corinthians 6:19-20; Romans 8:11). It is the indwelling of the Holy Spirit that continues to work in us both to will and to do God's pleasure (Philippians 2:13). The indwelling Spirit applies Christ's salvation to our daily lives, he produces the fruit of the Spirit within us (Galatians 5:22), and he sanctifies us for Christ's purpose for us in this life (Ephesians 2:10). It is God's mighty power administered to us by the Holy Spirit that enables us to say ,"No" (cries and tears), to the desires of our 'sin nature' for sinful, immoral lusts of the flesh. It is this power available to us that helps us live the victorious life in Christ. (Ephesians 1:19)

Chapter 9

~ *How Do I Live by the Spirit?* ~

~ *The Need* ~

I am always amused by the many Christians today who voice the desire to go back to the first century Church era, thinking that the Gospel at that time was perfect, that the worship of God was pure and blameless and simple, and that the Holy Spirit was more involved in a Christian's daily life than he is today. Well, maybe the Holy Spirit did seem to be more involved in what was going on in the first-century Church than in the church of today, but the operative word in this sentence is "seem".

If you were a Christian in the first century Church, you had to contend with the believers who belonged to the party of the Pharisees and who wanted to reintroduce 'obedience to the Law' into Paul's gospel of Grace (Acts 15:5; Galatians 1:6-9). Even the Ephesians, where Paul himself had spent over two years teaching (Acts 19:10), had lost their 'love' for Christ (first love) and were contending with the evil practices of the Nicolaitans, which Christ himself hated (read Revelation Chapters 2 and 3). Some Christians in Pergamum were holding to the teaching of Balaam, which included sexual immorality, and others were holding to the teaching of the Nicolaitans. Some Christians in Thyatira were tolerating a 'prophetess' (called 'that woman Jezebel') who was misleading Christians in worship and leading them into sexual immorality and who would not repent from such sins. Others had 'learned' Satan's so-called 'deep secrets'—which does not lead to acceptable worship of Christ or our Heavenly Father. Most Christians in Sardis were pronounced spiritually dead by our Lord, and Christians in Laodicea were so wretched, pitiful, poor, blind, and naked (in the spiritual sense) that our Lord was about to 'spit them out of his mouth' (Revelation 3:15-17). The Apostle Paul, in his letter to the Galatians, was, as usual, struggling with Christians about 'doctrine' (read 'basis for your faith'), and they just 'didn't seem to get it'! He wrote:

> *You, my brothers, were called to be free. But do not use your freedom to indulge the sinful nature; rather, serve one another in love. The entire law is summed up in a single command: "Love your neighbor as yourself." If you keep on biting and devouring each other, watch out or you will be destroyed by each other. So I say, live by the Spirit, and you will not gratify the desires of the sinful nature.*
> (Galatians 5:13-16)

Christians who would like to go back to the first century Church may have good intentions, but they lack knowledge, because they are not students of the Scriptures or of history. However, the solution now, even as then, is that we learn to 'live by the Spirit'. The sin nature that caused so many problems in the first century is the same sin nature that is causing so many problems in the twenty-first century. Living by the Spirit was necessary then, and it is necessary today, as well. The question that needs to be answered is, "How do I live by the Spirit?"

~ The Problem Identified ~

One of my first thoughts as a Christian was that I would be able to live the Christian life by my own determination and ability. I had made it through college and USAF pilot training on my own, and I felt that I had enough determination to do just about anything that I set my mind to do. Have you ever heard that statement? If you have heard such a statement and if you are like I was—I was determined to live the Christian life in my own strength and in my own power—you may think it is possible to do so on your own, as well. Anyway, no one had ever told me that such a thing was impossible. I liked the saying, "I will do the difficult today and I will complete the impossible by tomorrow!" Is that self-confidence or not? I had the right attitude, so I gave myself an "A" for attitude and desire, but as time went on I realized that even my attitude and desire seemed to have a mind of their own, and I found out that all my power was unable to control even me. A scriptural understanding was needed in order to know the problem and that the problem can only be solved by 'living by the Spirit'. The Apostle Paul addressed the problem and the solution with the Galatians. He said: *"For the sinful nature desires what is contrary to the Spirit, and the Spirit what is contrary to the sinful nature. They are in conflict with each other, so that you do not do what you want"* (Galatians 5:17).

~ Kill the Sin Nature ~

We all have a sinful nature that we received from Adam when he sinned in the Garden of Eden against God's command to him. Scripture tells us that we are slaves to this sinful nature, which is to say that the sinful nature dictates its desires to us and we by our own strength are not powerful enough to say "no", even if in our heart we want to say no. Paul also tells us, *"The sinful mind* (read desires of the sin nature) *is hostile to God. It does not submit to God's law, nor can it do so. Those controlled by the sinful nature cannot please God"* (Romans 8:7-8). In this, Paul is telling us that our sin nature has never been brought to obedience to God and that our sin nature has never and will never be obedient to God's will. Our sin nature is not able to be rehabilitated, and it can only be put to death—and must be put to death if we are to have eternal life. There are only two ways to put the sin nature to death. It can be put to death with Christ on the Cross (Romans 6:6; our 'old self' is our sin nature). *"For we know that our old self was crucified with him* (Christ) *so that the body of sin might be done away with, that we should no longer be slaves to sin."* The second way to put the sin nature to death is to take it with you as you are cast into the Lake of Fire, which is the second death, and it lasts eternally. *"Then death and Hades were thrown into the lake of fire. The lake of fire is the second death. If anyone's name was not found written in the book of life, he was thrown into the lake of fire"* (Revelation 20:14-15). It does not take a rocket scientist to figure out the best way to kill your 'sin nature', but I am amazed at the number of people who are willing to take it with them into the lake of fire rather than have it crucified (put to death) on the cross with Christ. Think about it.

It is only through the power of the Holy Spirit dwelling in us that we are able to say "no" to our sinful nature. I hope you are beginning to see the inner struggle that goes on within the heart (read mind) of the Christian. The sin nature is contrary to the Spirit, and the Spirit is contrary to the sinful nature. Both are within us—and it is "us" that determines which side will control the situation. The Apostle Paul shared with us his struggle in this matter.

> *We know that the law is spiritual; but I am unspiritual, sold as a slave to sin. I do not understand what I do. For what I want to do I do not do, but what I hate I do. And if I do what I do not want to do, I agree that the law is good. As it is, it is no longer I myself who do it, but it is sin living in me. I know that nothing good lives in me, that is, in my sinful nature. For I have the desire to do what is good, but I cannot carry it out. For what I do is not the good I want to do; no, the evil I do not want to do—this I keep on doing. Now if I do what I do not want to do, it is no longer I who do it, but it is sin living in me that does it.* (Romans 7:14-20)

If this was the 'living' condition for the Christian, it would be a pitiful situation in which to exist. Life would be one long frustration in not being able to stop doing what you did not want to do. This is not a problem for non-Christians, because they like to live a sinful lifestyle, because it pleases their sin natures. You might say, "I'm not a Christian, and my life is not so bad!" Paul lists some of the characteristics of the sinful life style—see if you fit in somewhere. *"The acts of the sinful nature are obvious: sexual immorality, impurity and debauchery; idolatry and witchcraft; hatred, discord, jealousy, fits of rage, selfish ambition, dissensions, factions and envy; drunkenness, orgies, and the like. I warn you, as I did before, that those who live like this will not inherit the kingdom of God"* (Galatians 5:19-21).

You may be involved in one or two, or several of these things, or even many of these things—and you may say that you enjoy them. It has never been said that there is no pleasure in sin, because there is—it is just that God will not put up with such things and let you into heaven. You may not like the consequence of living this way, which is to be thrown into the lake of fire—but you do not control the consequence of a sinful lifestyle.

~ The Solution Part One ~

Paul concluded his earlier comments with a solution to the problem.

> *So I find this law at work: When I want to do good, evil is right there with me. For in my inner being I delight in God's law; but I see another law at work in the members of my body, waging war against the law of my mind and making me a prisoner of the law of sin at work within my members. What a wretched man I am! Who will rescue me from this body of death? Thanks be to God—through Jesus Christ our Lord!"* (Romans 7:21-25)

It is a war! It is an ongoing struggle! But you can have victory in your life! When you accept Christ as your Lord and Savior, you are given a gift from Christ, which is the indwelling Holy Spirit. It is the Holy Spirit that enables your 'spirit' to say 'no' to your 'sin nature'. God's mighty power is made available to you as you 'remain in Christ' (John 15:5-8) and that will enable for you to overcome sin (Ephesians 1:19; 1 Corinthians 10:12-13). There may be (will be) failures, but as you grow as a Christian you will develop a stronger and stronger desire (Philippians 2:13) to be pleasing to your loving Heavenly Father by not sinning. In this way, you love and honor him.

~ A Review ~

We need to be very clear about who has a sin nature and who has the Spirit. Every human being has a sin nature that causes him/her to do sinful things. The sin nature that dwells within the human soul is exactly the same for every human being. Our personalities are different from each other but our sin nature is exactly the same for everyone. Our sin nature will attack us according to our different personalities but the tragic results is the same in every case—death and hell if we are not saved by the grace of God.

Things such as hatred, discord, jealousy, selfish ambition, dissensions, factions and envy are from the sin nature, as well as things such as drunkenness, sexual immorality, witchcraft, and the like. (Galatians 5:19-21). Not all of these things are continuously done in the unbeliever (read those who have not accepted Jesus Christ as their Lord and Savior), but at least one and maybe several of these will be a constant problem. Unbelievers have a sin nature, but they do not have the Spirit of God living in them. There is no struggle in their hearts (read mind) against doing any of the above things, and at least one of the above, and likely more, will be consistent as their lifestyle. No unbeliever will make it to heaven. (Galatians 5:21).

The person who has accepted Christ as Savior and Lord of his/her life (read a Christian) not only is saved (read will go to heaven) but also is given the Holy Spirit to dwell within him/her, to empower him/her to say "no" to the sinful desires of the sin nature. However, even though the Holy Spirit dwells within the believer, the believer has a responsibility to be obedient to the leading and convicting of the Holy Spirit. The Christian must be submissive and obedient—no matter what the cost of obedience. This is not an easy thing to do, because our sin nature cries out to satisfy the 'lusts of the flesh'; that is a common desire to all of us. If the Holy Spirit did not help us when we submit to him, we could never say 'no' to sin.

~ Any Help for the Unbeliever? ~

The question might be asked, "Does the Spirit do anything for the unbeliever?" The answer is, "Yes!" The Spirit does several things for the unbeliever. The Spirit will strive against the sinfulness of the unbeliever. (Genesis 6:3; 2 Thessalonians 2:7). He does this through the conscience and the innate knowledge of 'good' and 'evil' common within every human being. He sometimes does this through 'civil authority', such as the laws that have been made and law enforcement officials who enforce those laws. The Holy Spirit also convicts unbelievers of their need to repent of their sins and turn to Jesus for salvation. This is what has happened to every believer. It is the Holy Spirit who draws people (unbelievers) to Christ. For those who are still sensitive to 'good' and 'evil', the Holy Spirit convicts of guilt and judgment against sin and of a need for forgiveness.

~ The Fruit of the Spirit ~

Part of 'living by the Spirit' is cooperation with the Holy Spirit as he produces 'fruit' (read God's characteristics) within the believer. Paul lists the characteristics for us in Galatians 5:22. *"But the fruit of the Spirit is love, joy, peace, patience, kindness, goodness, faithfulness, gentleness and self-control."* These are characteristics of people who are not 'biting and devouring each other', and those who do 'bite and devour' each other do not exhibit these characteristics as a lifestyle. The problem is that even Christians, such as those to whom the Apostle Paul was writing, were using their 'freedom' to indulge the sinful nature, rather than to serve one another in love. God expects better of his 'children' than to do this; however, he will let us do what we want, but not without consequences. Paul told the Galatians in the next chapter (Galatians 6:7), *"Do not be deceived: God cannot be mocked. A man reaps what he sows. The one who sows to please his sinful nature, from that nature will reap destruction; . . ."*. The Apostle goes on to say, *"Let us not become weary in doing good, for at the proper time we will reap a harvest if we do not give up"* (Verse 9). It is easy for us to give up and start being ugly—which so pleases our sin nature. However, if we do, we are setting ourselves up for discipline from our Heavenly Father. *"My son* (children), *do not make light of the Lord's discipline, and do not lose heart when he rebukes you, because the Lord disciplines those he loves, and he punishes everyone he accepts as a son* (child)*"* (Hebrews 12:5b-6).

Many Christians are suffering hardship and do not realize it is just discipline from our Heavenly Father (Hebrews 12:7). The more our willfulness—the more the discipline, so we must test our own actions (Galatians 6:4). There are some 'Christians' who have been so self-willed that they have hardly had an enjoyable day in their Christian life. Paul encouraged the Ephesians *"to live a life worthy of the calling you have received. Be completely humble and gentle; be patient, bearing with one another in love. Make every effort to keep the unity of the Spirit through the bond of peace"* (Ephesians 4:1b-3). It is not possible to be a narcissist (self-centered person) and a pleasing Christian at the same time.

~ *The Solution Part Two* ~

The solution to 'living by the Spirit' is to be empowered by the Spirit and to be obedient to the leading of the Spirit in our lives, for it is the Spirit who works in us both to 'will' and to 'do' the will of God. *"[F]or it is God who works in you to will and to act according to his good purpose"* (Philippians 2:13).

Paul wrote to the Ephesians:

> *. . . and his incomparably great power for us who believe. That power is like the working of his mighty strength, which he exerted in Christ when he raised him from the dead and seated him at his right hand in the heavenly realms, far above all rule and authority, power and dominion, and every title that can be given, not only in the present age but also in the one to come. And God placed all things under his feet and appointed him to be head over everything for the church, which is his body, the fullness of him who fills everything in every way.* (Ephesians 1:19-23)

The Apostle Paul continued to instruct the Galatians. *"But if you are led by the Spirit, you are not under law"* (Galatians 5:18). In his letter to the Romans, Paul stated: *"For sin shall not be your master, because you are not under law, but under grace"* (Romans 6:14). The law condemns us when we sin. We need to only sin one time to be a 'law breaker' and be condemned to 'death' by the law. But, grace does not condemn us, even when we sin! But because we have been placed into Christ by baptism (the baptism of the Holy Spirit when we are placed into the body of Christ—the church, therefore with him into his death, at the same time the Holy Spirit comes to dwell within us—1 Corinthians 12:13; Romans 6:3-4, we are now to count ourselves dead to sin but alive to God in Christ Jesus. (Romans 6:11). Therefore, we are to no longer be slaves to sin—because anyone who has died (with Christ on the cross) has been freed from sin (legally-before God).

The problem here is that our Heavenly Father "sees" us, through the Spirit's baptism of placing us in Christ and his death and resurrection, as having died with Christ, having been resurrected with Christ, and already glorified with him. But our 'physical experience' says that we are still alive and suffer with a sin nature. This is to say that our 'spiritual position' before God is different from our 'physical experience' at the present moment. They will not be the same, until we actually die physically. In the meantime, the Holy Spirit is working to make our 'physical experience' as much like our 'spiritual position' as possible. This is a process called sanctification, and it continues until we are physically dead. The sanctification process is the Holy Spirit helping us to have power over the sin nature that would control our lives. It is a process by which we live in victory over ungodliness (read wickedness of sin) and live pleasingly before our Heavenly Father, who is our great reward. Life on earth lasts only a short time—eternity lasts forever!

God's mighty power is available to us as we live by the Spirit and are led by the Spirit. We can not do it on our own. My friend, Vicky Odundo, who runs a children's orphanage in Kenya, Africa, prays that we know Christ who will give:

PEACE for every struggle,
SUPPLY for every need,
SOLUTION for every problem,
ESCAPE for every temptation,
RELEASE for every burden,
BALM for every pain,
COMFORT for every sorrow,
VICTORY for every battle,
WISDOM for every decision,
STRENGTH for every endeavor,
HOPE for every tomorrow,
A SONG for every day!

So, just as the first-century Christians lived by the Spirit, so do Christians today. Living by the Spirit has its great advantages and blessings in our daily lives, even now, and will result in a great reward in eternity (1 Corinthians 3:10-15). The Lord Jesus is going to reward us for our faithful service to him as we serve and love others, which includes everyone—not just Christians, with the help of the Holy Spirit.

Chapter 10

~ *What Do You Know About Resurrections and Judgments?* ~

In the Christian community, questions concerning resurrections and judgments are generally limited to *timing* and *location* of events, not whether there will be a resurrection and judgment in our future. The questions of a pre-tribulation, post-tribulation, or mid-tribulation resurrection and rapture of the church or the pre-millennial, post-millennial or a millennial return of Christ to the earth are in-house discussions within the Christian community. There is common agreement that there will be a return of Christ, that there will be a resurrection, and that there will be a judgment. The scriptures are quite plain about these things. While timing of events can generally be determined, the Scriptures do not directly address the issue of timing, and concerning the return of Christ specifically states that no one knows the 'day or the hour.' If we can determine the 'season', we would do well—but a lot of people have been wrong about this, also. It has been nearly two thousand years since Christ promised to return and the only thing we can say for sure is that we are nearly two thousand years closer to the return of Christ than were the first-century Christians.

~ All kinds of people ~

I will define various groups of people, so that we can know whom we are discussing.

- Scripturally, there are two basic groups—Jews and Gentiles. If you are not a Jew, you are a Gentile. White, yellow, black, or brown makes no difference; if you are not Jewish, you are a Gentile.
- The 'Church'. The Church is made up of believers, Jews or Gentiles, who have come to Christ (Christ, of course, draws us to himself), confessed their sins, accepted Christ's forgiveness and have received the free gift of eternal life and the indwelling Holy Spirit. If this has, in fact, happened, then the Holy Spirit places the believers into the 'body' of Christ, which is the 'Church.' It is the Holy Spirit who places believers into the body of Christ. (1 Corinthians 12:13). The Church is made up of believers from the beginning of the Church at Pentecost until the rapture or removal of the Church from the earth. The Church does not include Old Testament believers or Tribulation Saints, even though they are believers and their names are in the Lamb's book of Life.
- The 'visible church.' The visible church is made up of the 'Church' and all others who incorrectly claim church membership, such as cults like the Jehovah Witnesses, Mormons, etc., and those who attend a church yet are not Christians. The visible church is always much larger than the real or true Church. Many may be very 'religious' but are not Christians.
- The unbeliever. The unbeliever is a person who has not come to Christ for forgiveness of sins. This group includes those who are very much against Christ, those who just do not want Christ in their life and those who pretend to be believers but really are not. It is this last group that causes a lot of problems in the church. Also among the unbelievers, are those who have not yet come to Christ for salvation but will do so sometime during their life. These are the ones that we seek for salvation and, of course, we do not know who they are. Those who remain unbelievers until they die physically are grouped together with every other unbeliever from the beginning of the human race until the end of the Millennial Kingdom of Christ. They consist of one very large group.

- The Old Testament believer. The Old Testament believer has his name in the Lamb's Book of Life, therefore, has eternal life, but is not a member of the Church.
- Tribulation Saints. Many Gentiles will be saved during the tribulation. They will not be members of the Church, because the Church Age will have been closed upon the removal of the Church from the earth prior to the beginning of the tribulation. This is the pre-tribulation view of the Church. The Tribulation Saints are not considered along with Old Testament believers either, but are a special group and are addressed in the book of Revelation.
- Jews saved during the Tribulation. Jews who are saved during the tribulation are included along with the Jews who are saved in the dispensation of the Old Testament. The seven years of the tribulation are just the last seven years of the Old Testament dispensation. The Church age is a parenthetical length of time inserted between Daniel's 69th week of years and the 70th week as described in Daniel 9:20-27 and is not a part of the Old Testament dispensation but rather a separate dispensation of Grace known as the Church age.

~ *The Scriptural Voice on Salvation, Judgments, and Resurrection* ~

Jesus is recorded in John 5:24-29 as saying these words:

> *I tell you the truth, whoever hears my words and believes him who sent me has eternal life and will not be condemned* [judged-KJV]; *he has crossed over from death to life. I tell you the truth, a time is coming and has now come when the dead will hear the voice of the Son of God and those who hear will live. For as the Father has life in himself, so he has granted the Son to have life in himself. And he* [The Father] *has given him* [the Son] *authority to judge because he is the Son of Man. Do not be amazed at this, for a time is coming when all who are in their graves will hear his voice and come out—those who have done good will rise to live, and those who have done evil will rise to be condemned. By myself I can do nothing; I judge only as I hear, and my judgment is just, for I seek not to please myself but him who sent me.*

At the time Christ said this (Verse 25), people (the spiritually dead—not the physically dead) were hearing his voice, and many believed in him and were being granted eternal life (to live). John the Baptist was one of these individuals who believed in Christ, was certainly awarded eternal life, and yet remained one of the Old Testament believers and did not become a member of the 'Church.' The Church was started on the day of Pentecost, some fifty days after the resurrection of Christ and a few years after John was beheaded by Herod.

Everyone will eventually hear a command to rise and will come out of their graves for judgment. As we shall see from other Scriptures, there is not a common, one-time resurrection in which everyone is resurrected at the same time. Remember that it is the physical body that is in the grave that will be resurrected. The soul and spirit of the unbeliever is, upon physical death, incarcerated in Sheol (Hebrew) or Hades (Greek), translated hell in the King James Version. Their souls and spirits will remain in Hades until the command comes for them to be raised for judgment. The soul and spirit of the believer goes to the Paradise side of Sheol (Luke 16:19-31), which was a very nice place to be, but they were held prisoner there until Christ would pay for their sins, so that they could be released to go to heaven. They were taken to heaven when Christ ascended to heaven after his resurrection. (2 Corinthians 12:2-4; compare Luke 4:18c and Ephesians 4:8). The Paradise side of Sheol is now in the 'third heaven' in the presence of Christ. In this present age of grace, the soul and spirit of the believer, upon physical death, goes directly to be with the Lord in heaven. Therefore, for the believer, to be absent from the body is to be present with the Lord (2 Corinthians 5:8). We also need to understand that, for everyone—believer and unbeliever alike—the soul and spirit do not die as the physical body dies and corrupts. Neither does the soul and spirit 'age'—it does not grow older, weaker, or corrupt (deteriorate), etc.

It may seem from John 5: 28 that there is a "one-time resurrection" for everyone, good or bad, saved and lost, to face a common judgment. This is not the case, as we shall see. It may also seem from Verse 29 that the key to "live" was to have "done good" in their lives and not evil. We must also understand this verse by comparing it to other verses. You can consider the "done good" to mean to believe on the Lord Jesus for salvation, not on any accomplishments of "good works" to earn salvation.

We can understand this by looking at Ephesians 2:8-9. *"For it is by grace you have been saved, through faith—and this not from yourselves, it is the gift of God—not by works, so that no one can boast."* As Christians, we are to do good works, but not as a means to earn our salvation. We read in Ephesians 2:10: *"For we are God's workmanship, created in Christ Jesus to do good works, which God prepared in advance for us to do."*

God's plan and purpose for us is to be saved by grace through faith in Christ Jesus and then to become available to him to do good works, which he has prepared in advance for us to do. This is true no matter what our vocation, for everyone should be a believer and obedient to the Will of the Father. Wouldn't that make for a great world? God's plan and purpose for Christians is important when considering our judgment.

Taking John 5:24-29 one verse at a time, we see there are five things that we want to learn from the passage about resurrection and judgment for believers, as well as the unbeliever. First, Jesus Christ is the judge for everyone. Second, those who hear and believe Christ are given eternal life and will not be condemned—ever! Third, eternal life begins immediately upon believing in Christ as Savior. Fourth, everyone—not just believers—will be resurrected. Fifth, Jesus Christ will do all judging as pleases the Father.

First, as for Jesus Christ being the judge for everyone, God the Father has put all judgment into the hands of Christ, the God-man. The Apostle Paul confirms this in Acts 17: 31, when he is speaking concerning the judgment. *"For he* [God the Father] *has set a day when he will judge the world with justice by the man he has appointed. He has given proof of this to all men by raising him from the dead."* Paul said these words during a debate at the Areopagus, speaking to the men of Athens, Epicurean and Stoic philosophers, who had, along with all the altars to their pagan gods, an altar to the 'Unknown God.' Paul was telling them about their 'Unknown God.' If you think you have ever had a difficult time witnessing to anyone, consider Paul who was witnessing to professional debaters with a pagan worldview.

The Epicureans followed the philosophy of Epicurus who subscribed to a hedonistic ethic that considered an imperturbable emotional call the highest good and whose followers held intellectual pleasures superior to transient sensualism. The Stoics were members of a school of philosophy founded by Zeno of Citium about 300 B.C., who believed that the wise man should be free from passion, unmoved by joy or grief, and submissive to natural law, apparently, or professedly, indifferent to pleasure or pain. Another Greek philosophy was Hedonism, the doctrine that pleasure or happiness is the sole or chief good in life. Thus, physical pleasures of any kind were okay for them, which is not accepted by the Scriptures, because some physical pleasures are defined as sin or lust of the flesh, as in Galatians 5:19-21. None of these philosophies can lead to salvation.

The Apostle Paul, because of whom he was addressing, was just establishing the fact that the Creator God (their Unknown God) had a day, or an appointed at time, in which he was going to judge all things, and that he had a specific individual who was going to be the judge. Paul was not trying to explain the details concerning the judgment, such as the amount of time it would take, or exactly when it would occur.

Second, in speaking of receiving eternal life, we need to look at John 5:24. *"I tell you the truth, whoever hears my word and believes him* [God the Father] *who sent me* [Christ] *has eternal life and will not be condemned* [judged]*; he has crossed over from death to life."* And third, the crossing over from death to life happens for us at the time belief (faith) is placed in the word of Christ. This is the plan and purpose of the Father. We are not the ones to determine who receives faith and when faith is placed in Christ. God is the one who determines this, and it is God who gives eternal life. (John 3:16). *"I tell you the truth, a time is coming and has now come when the dead will hear the voice of the Son of God and those who hear will live. For as the Father has life in himself, so he has granted the Son to have life in himself. And he has given him authority to judge because he is the Son of Man"* (John 5: 25-27).

These three verses are not directly connected to a resurrection. They deal with people who have the 'ears' (heart) to hear and, therefore, believe and receive 'life.' It is to be understood that this 'life' will last forever, which is to say eternal life. We are given eternal life and have eternal life even though our physical bodies will die. Our spirit and soul will be eternally alive, because the soul and spirit do not die. 2 Corinthians 5:8: *"We are confident, I say, and would prefer to be away from the body and at home with the Lord.* (NIV). *"We are confident, I say, and willing rather to be absent from the body, and to be present with the Lord."* (KJV).

Those who believe in several lives (reincarnation) are under the influence of a lie—right out of the pit of hell—from Satan himself. There is only one life for each to live, and only one physical death. *"Just as man is destined to die <u>once</u>, but after that to face judgment . . ."* (Hebrews 9:27). Those who were raised from the dead in the Bible died again, and those who have 'near death' experiences still have only one life to live and one permanent death that will end their physical life.

Fourth, in regard to the resurrection, Christ declares that everyone will be resurrected—not just the believers. John 5:28-29. *"Do not be amazed at this, for a time is coming when all who are in their graves will hear his voice and come out—those who have done good will rise to live, and those who have done evil will rise to be condemned"* (John 5:28-29). And fifth, as far as the judgment goes, Jesus goes on to say, *"By myself I can do nothing; I judge only as I hear, and my judgment is just, for I seek not to please myself but him who sent me"* (John 5:30). Christ has subordinated himself to do the Will of the Father, to the point that he does nothing on his own—he is totally obedient to the Father's Will. All of the attributes of the Godhead belong to Christ, as well as to the Father and the Holy Spirit, but Christ has subordinated himself to the plans and purpose of the Father. When Christ judges, it will be to please the Father. Christ is to be our example; we too should subordinate ourselves to do the Will of the Father and to please him in all that we do. God has, in the Scriptures, given us commands by which to live. We should seek God's Will, with the purpose of obedience. God leads us through the Holy Spirit.

~ Resurrections ~

The 'first resurrection' is a term (Revelation 20:5-6) for the resurrection of everyone who has been given eternal life. The 'first resurrection' occurs in a series of resurrections and, therefore, they do not all occur at the same time. Christ was the "First Fruits" of what is called the first resurrection. Paul addresses this in 1 Corinthians 15:20-23.

> *But Christ has indeed been raised from the dead, the first fruits of those who have fallen asleep* (died physically). *For since death came through a man, the resurrection of the dead comes also through a man. For as in Adam all die, so in Christ all* (believers in Christ) *will be made alive. <u>But each in his own turn</u>: Christ, the first fruits; then, when he comes, those who belong to him.*

Christ, who was resurrected some two thousand years ago, was the "first fruits" of the 'first resurrection.' Christ's resurrection as 'first fruits' was a visual promise that we too would be resurrected like him someday. The resurrection of the church will also be part of the 'first resurrection' but will obviously not be at the same time as Christ. There will be at least some two thousand years that will separate our (the Church's) resurrection and that of Christ. The resurrection for the Church will occur at the time of the 'rapture' of the Church. Old Testament believers and the Tribulation Saints are also part of the 'first resurrection', but they are not resurrected until after the tribulation is over. This will put their resurrection at least seven years (the length of the tribulation) after the resurrection (rapture) of the Church.

Those who belong to Christ, when he comes, are the Church. "When he comes" is when Christ comes for the Church, and we meet him in the "air." Christ does not come all the way back to the earth at the rapture (1

Thessalonians 4:13-17). Christ does not come all the way back to earth until the end of the tribulation, at which time he will set up his millennial kingdom (Matthew 25:31-46; Revelation 19:11-16; 20:5-6). It is also at this time that Christ will judge the nations (Matthew 25:31-46). This judgment of the nations is for entry into the millennial kingdom. Those judged not fit to enter the kingdom are cast directly into the 'lake of fire', which is the second death, or eternal hell (Revelation 20:11-15). Those nations (peoples) who live through the tribulation are judged as to whether or not they can be a part of Christ's direct rule for the 1,000 years (millennium = 1,000) millennial kingdom.

~ *The Rapture* ~

The word 'rapture' is not in the Scriptures, but the event is perfectly described for us in 1 Thessalonians 4:13-18.

> *Brothers, we do not want you to be ignorant about those who fall asleep* [those who have died physically], *or to grieve like the rest of men, who have no hope. We believe that Jesus died and rose again and so we believe that God will bring with Jesus those who have fallen asleep in him. According to the Lord's own word, we tell you that we who are still alive, who are left till the coming of the Lord, will certainly not precede those who have fallen asleep. For the Lord himself will come down from heaven, with a loud command, with the voice of the archangel and with the trumpet call of God, and the dead in Christ will rise first. After that, we who are still alive and are left will be caught up together with them in the clouds to meet the Lord in the air. And so we will be with the Lord forever. Therefore encourage each other with these words.*

Paul shared a mystery with the Corinthians about the rapture. It was called a mystery only because we were not aware of it before—not because we could not understand it.

> *"Listen, I tell you a mystery: We will not all sleep, but we will all be changed—in a flash, in the twinkling of an eye, at the last trumpet. For the trumpet will sound, the dead will be raised imperishable, and we will be changed. For the perishable must cloth itself with the imperishable, and the mortal with immortality"* (1 Corinthians 15:51-53).

Sometimes it is confusing when the 'last trumpet' is mentioned. The last trumpet for the church is not to be confused with the seventh (last) trumpet judgment of Revelation. Those who consider them the same believe that the 'church' is raptured at that time—which would be mid-tribulation.

When the rapture of the Church occurs, those who are alive at that time will be changed from their mortal bodies to their immortal bodies. It will take place in a flash—in the twinkling of an eye. The twinkling of an eye is described as the time it takes light to travel through the cornea of the eye. The cornea is the transparent part of the coat of the eyeball that covers the iris and pupil and admits light to enter the interior of the eye. Light travels at 186,000 miles per second (around the world 7 ½ times per second), so you can only imagine how quick the twinkling of the eye is and how fast God will change us to our immortal bodies. If you are a pre-tribulationist, which I am, you understand that this event precedes the tribulation. Note also that this resurrection is for the 'church' only. It does not include Old Testament believers, the Tribulation Saints, or unbelievers.

~ The Jews ~

Because Christ deals with the Jews during the tribulation, they are not resurrected until after the tribulation. The 144,000 Jews from the tribes that were marked [Revelation 7:1-8] will be a 'first fruits' of the 'tribulation'. *"And they sang a new song before the throne and before the four living creatures and the elders. No one could learn the song except the 144,000 who had been redeemed from the earth. . . . They were purchased from among men and offered as first fruits to God and the Lamb"* (Revelation 14:3, 4c).

The 144,000 thousand Jews are not the only Jews saved during the tribulation, but they are considered the 'first fruits' of the tribulation. These 144,000 Jews will be witnesses and 'evangelists' for Christ during the Tribulation and are marked for special protection from the Antichrist. Many Jews are saved during the tribulation and are resurrected at the end of the tribulation, along with the rest of the Old Testament believers.

The seven years of the tribulation are, in fact, the last seven years of the Old Testament dispensation. The New Testament dispensation is a parenthetical time inserted into the seventy weeks of years spoken of by Daniel (Daniel 9:20-27). The church age or the age of grace was established after Christ was crucified (the Anointed One will be cut off, Daniel 9:26). The nation of Israel, as a whole, had rejected Christ as the Messiah. Paul addresses this in the eleventh chapter of Romans. When the full number of Gentiles has come in, God will again deal with Israel (Acts 15:16-18). The full number of Gentiles will have been accomplished at the rapture of the Church (Romans 11: 25). God will then deal with Israel again, that is, during the last seven years known as the tribulation (Acts 15:14-18).

The various resurrections of the righteous are all considered part of the 'first resurrection.' Blessed are those who are part of the first resurrection Revelation 20:6). Unbelievers are not resurrected for another thousand years or until after the one thousand year reign of Christ on earth has passed. All those who remain 'unbelievers' during the Kingdom reign of Christ will be put together with all unbelievers from the time of 'Cain'. They will all be resurrected as one group for judgment at the Great White Throne judgment (Revelation 20:11-15).

~ Judging the Nations ~

Christ's judging the nations is not to be considered as part of the final judgment, i.e. the Great White Throne judgment. The judgment of the nations is not an uncommon type of judgment and is consistent with God's judgment throughout human history. God's judgment on people is a reality of normal, everyday, divine judgment, and while consistent with God's divine judgment that will end all things, that is the Bema Seat judgment and the Great White Throne judgment, these judgments are not to be thought of as the final judgment for either believers or unbelievers. God judged Adam and Eve, expelling them from the Garden and pronouncing curses on their future earthly life and ours as well (Gen 3). God judged the sinful, ungodly people of Noah's time, killing them with a flood. God judged the sinful people of Sodom and Gomorrah, killing them with burning sulfur from heaven (Gen 18-19). God judged Egypt for their harsh treatment of the Israelites, killing some of them in the Red Sea (Gen 15:14; Exodus 7-12). God judged those who worshiped the golden calf, killing three thousand with the sword (Exodus 32:26-26). God judged Nadab and Abihu, killing them for offering strange fire (Leviticus 10:1-3). God judged Korah, Dathan, and Abiram, killing them by being swallowed up by the earth; God judged the unbelieving Hebrews whom he had just brought out of Egypt when they refused, because of a lack of faith, to go in and take the land promised by God for them. All over twenty years (except Joshua and Caleb) died in the wilderness (Numbers 13-14). God judged Achan for thievery, killing him and all of his family; God judged Israel for their unfaithfulness to him; He judged the Northern ten tribes—carrying them off to Syrian captivity—killing many; God judged Judah and Benjamin with captivity in Babylon—killing many; God judged Nebuchadnezzar and Belshazzar; God judged Ananias and Sapphira—that they died, and Herod, who was struck dead, and Elymas who was struck blind (Acts 13:8-11). God inflicted sickness and even death on some of the Corinthians because of their behavior at the communion supper (1 Corinthians 11:27-30). Christ judges anti-Semitism during the tribulation.

The judgment of the nations takes place when Christ returns to earth in glory, with his angels, as he establishes his millennial kingdom. This judgment occurs at the end of the Tribulation and concerns those who have survived the Tribulation, but some are not believers in Christ. The righteous, whose works demonstrated their faith (James 2:26) and love, are invited into the millennial kingdom. The unrighteous are judged and immediately assigned to the Lake of Fire. The cause of this action is that during the tribulation, the spiritual battle that rages unseen in this age is not unseen then, but is very visual—with God and his angels in drastic events and in open warfare and judgment upon Satan and demons, especially in the last three and one half years. Anti-Semitism will be at an all time high because Satan, who initiates anti-Semitism—even now, will be directly involved. Everyone knows what is happening. (Revelation 6:15-17). God will judge those nations because of their treatment of the Jews (his brethren), fulfilling prophesy given to Abraham when he was called by God (Genesis 12:2-3). We, the United States, need to be very careful and not be anti-Semitic, or we too will be judged for that sin.

This judgment occurs over a thousand years before the judgment of the Great White Throne. The throne that Christ is sitting on (Matthew 25:31) is his kingdom throne—not the Great White Throne of judgment. Since the 'Church' has been removed from earth and is in heaven during this time—this judgment has nothing to do with Christians or the Church. At the end of the millennial kingdom, shortly after Satan has been released to deceive the nations for a final time, the nations react by rebelling against Christ's rule, surround Jerusalem, and are judged by Christ with fire from heaven—devouring them (Revelation 20:7-10, Psalm 2). The wrath of God is being revealed (on a continuous basis) against all the godlessness and wickedness of men who suppress the truth by their wickedness (Romans 1:18). The judging of the nations (Matthew 25:31-46) is just one of many judgments.

~ *The Second Resurrection* ~

The resurrection of unbelievers is called the second resurrection. Those in the second resurrection will be gathered for judgment at the Great White Throne. John saw and recorded this as found in Revelation 20:4-6.

> *I saw thrones on which were seated those who had been given authority to judge. And I saw the souls of those who had been beheaded because of their testimony for Jesus and because of the word of God. They had not worshiped the beast* [during the tribulation] *or his image and had not received his mark on their foreheads or their hands. They came to life and reigned with Christ a thousand years. (The rest of the dead* [unbelievers] d*id not come to life until the thousand years were ended.) This is the first resurrection. Blessed and holy are those who have part in the first resurrection. The second death has no power over them, but they will be priests of God and of Christ and will reign with him for a thousand years.*

It may have seemed from John 5:24-29 that there was a 'one-time' resurrection for everyone, good or bad, saved or lost, to face a common judgment time. As the Scriptures show, this is not the case.

~ *The Judgments* ~

When Jesus comes back to judge, he will not be observed as the suffering servant, as we saw him in the Gospels. He will return as the King of Kings and as the Lord of Lords who will judge and rule and reign. (Revelation 1:12-16; 19:11-13).

In Romans 2:16, the Apostle Paul is again speaking about judgment. *"This will take place on the day when God will judge men's secrets through Jesus Christ, as my gospel declares."* The "secrets" of men will be their thoughts and attitudes.

When my Number Two Princess, my second daughter, first learned that God knew our thoughts and attitudes, she thought that was a real bummer. But, I would not want a God from whom I could hide my thoughts. I am sure that I would always be trying not to let him know what I was thinking. It is a strong motivator to me to know that God knows my attitude, and he also knows everything I am thinking. My Number Two Princess feels the same way now.

Psalm 139:1-6 puts it this way:

> *O Lord, you have searched me and you know me. You know when I sit and when I rise; you perceive my thoughts from afar. You discern my going out and my lying down; you are familiar with all my ways. Before a word is on my tongue you know it completely, O Lord. You hem me in—behind and before; you have laid you hand upon me. Such knowledge is too wonderful for me, too lofty for me to attain.*

God's ability in this is really for our benefit. Verses 23-24 show how we can be blest by this. *"Search me, O God, and know my heart; test me and know my anxious thoughts. See if there is any offensive way in me, and lead me in the way everlasting."* Our loving Heavenly Father is able to do this for our good and will do so without condemning us in any way.

For the believer, this is truly a liberating benefit, but that is not true for the unbelievers. Hebrews 4:13 adds dread to the sinner. *"Nothing in all creation is hidden from God's sight. Everything is uncovered and laid bare before the eyes of him to whom we must give account."* Even though the unbeliever may think he has nothing to do with God, that is really not the case.

We must all remember that our Loving Heavenly Father is eager to forgive us our sins through Christ and to cleanse us from all unrighteousness. Then to lead—not drive us— in the way everlasting. The Apostle John shares with us God's desire in this. *"If we claim to be without sin, we deceive ourselves and the truth is not in us. If we confess our sins, he is faithful and just and will forgive us our sins and purify us from all unrighteousness"* (1 John 1:8-9).

I have experienced times when I have been angry, and I have not even wanted to confess my sins. But, after considering the love of God, I do confess my sins to God with the full knowledge that I will be forgiven and cleansed from all unrighteousness. This is not because of me, but it is because of a loving Heavenly Father who, in his grace, is faithful to me. With this knowledge, I am confident to face the judgment that is to come.

It is also comforting to know that judgment is for God to make—not us. Romans 14:10 states it this way:

> *You, then, why do you judge your brother? Or why do you look down on your brother? <u>For we will all stand before God's Judgment seat</u>. It is written: "As surely as I live," says the Lord, " every knee will bow before me; every tongue will confess to God." So then, each of us will give an account of himself to God.*

In this verse, the Apostle Paul is speaking to Christians only. It is only Christians who will appear before the "judgment seat" or "Bema Seat" of Christ. God's Judgment Seat here is translated from the "Bema Seat" of Christ. Non-believers, or non-Christians, do not appear at the Bema Seat; they will be judged at the "Great White Throne" as described in Revelation 20.

Furthermore, 2 Corinthians 5:10 confirms our judgment before Christ. *"For we must all appear before the judgment seat of Christ, that each one may receive what is due him for the things done while in the body, whether good or bad."* Paul is speaking here to the Christians in Corinth, not to 'all' people in general. The unbeliever can do nothing 'good' in the scriptural sense. John 15:5, where Jesus is speaking to the disciples, explains it this way. *"I am the vine; you are the branches. If a man remains in me and I in him, he will bear much fruit; apart from me you can do nothing."*

People, of course, can do worthwhile things as considered by the world, but they can not do things that will have an eternal value. Paul addresses this in 1 Corinthians 13:1-3.

> *If I speak in the tongues of men and of angels, but have not love, I am only a resounding gong or a clanging cymbal. If I have the gift of prophecy and can fathom all mysteries and all knowledge, and if I have a faith that can move mountains, but have not love, I am nothing. If I give all I possess to the poor and surrender my body to the flames, but have not love, I gain nothing.*

The love that Paul is talking about is "agape" love—or a self-sacrificing love. This love is produced within the believer by the Holy Spirit. The Holy Spirit dwells only in the believer. As believers, we are given the gift of the Holy Spirit to dwell within us—to apply Christ's salvation to our lives; to sanctify us to Christ's purpose; to convict us of sin in our lives, and to strengthen and comfort us. All the other kinds of love known to man are natural for humankind, but only those things done by the motivation of Christ's love within us and in obedience to Christ counts in an eternal way. This is totally foreign to the unbeliever, who, not being in Christ is unable to do anything good in Christ's eyes.

~The Lost and the Saved ~

It is important to understand that the judgment for the believer and the unbeliever does not involve a determination of being lost or saved.

The determination of being lost or saved is made while people are alive on earth, and before any judgment takes place. When a person believes and accepts Christ's atoning death, he/she is given the gift of eternal life at that moment. The unbeliever, who has never accepted Christ, has always been lost (John 3:17-21). This too is determined while living on earth. There is no second chance for the unbeliever to be saved after physical death from this world. Hebrews 9:27 states, *"Just as man is destined to die once, and after that to face judgment."* There is no such thing as reincarnation and many lives to live. Universalists who claim that 'all' or everyone will be saved do so by rejecting the plain word of Scripture because of their desire to have everyone saved. This may be a heartfelt desire but is totally unscriptural and will, if truly believed, be very harmful.

John 3:17-18 states: *"For God did not send his Son into the world to condemn the world, but to save the world through him. Whoever believes in him is not condemned, but whoever does not believe stands condemned already because he has not believed in the name of God's one and only Son."*

To be condemned is to be given over to eternal separation (which is eternal death) from God. Therefore, for the believer, eternal life is given as a gift from God upon belief in Christ Jesus. For the unbeliever, condemnation (eternal separation or eternal death) will have always been his position, because he has rejected (refused) Christ. Both of these positions are determined while alive on earth. Physical death terminates any decisions that could have been made in this respect. God respects people's decisions to reject him. If they continually reject him and refuse to come to him, then God simply honors that decision. The rejecter may not realize the terrible consequence to his decision, but the Holy Spirit will have convicted him of sin, and of righteousness, and of judgment (John 16:8)—he will be without excuse.

~ The Bema Seat ~

All the sins of the Christian have been forgiven and will not be addressed at the Bema Seat Judgment of Christ. Our sins have been removed (forgiven) and will not be shown on the 'big screen' for everyone to see.

Since salvation, being lost or saved is determined while alive on earth—it will not be addressed in the judgment for either the Christian or the unbeliever. For the Christian, sins have been forgiven and removed as far as the east is from the west (Psalm 103: 12)—so sins are not addressed at the Bema Seat judgment. So what will be addressed at the Bema Seat?

For the Christian, our works are the works that we were created in Christ Jesus to do. Remember Ephesians 2:10. *"For we are God's workmanship, created in Christ Jesus to do good works, which God prepared in advance for us to do."* To stress a point, these works are not to earn eternal life, which is a free gift to us by God's grace through our faith in Christ. Our works will be judged in order to determine what our reward will be to take into heaven.

I have referred to 1 John 1:8-9, and I want to clear up a point so that a misunderstanding does not occur. When the Christian confesses his sins and believes in Christ—all sins, past, present, and future, have already been forgiven. Christ died once for all sins. No sin has been left unforgiven. When we do sin after becoming a Christian, we do not lose our eternal life, but our fellowship with God can be interrupted and serious consequences can be experienced. We confess that sin (acknowledging it is sin) in order to remain in fellowship with God. We must acknowledge sin, as sin, when the Holy Spirit convicts us. We interrupt fellowship with God if we try to live with sin in our lives. God is faithful and just to forgive us our confessed sins and to cleanse us from all unrighteousness; though we may still suffer consequences of our sins temporally in this life, Christ paid for the eternal consequence. Confessing our sins restores fellowship with God and the joy of our salvation. Do not worry about dying in an accident, or to suddenly die with unconfessed sin being laid to your account—that will not happen.

The Arminian view of the forgiveness of sins is that not all sins are forgiven when a person accepts Christ as savior. They do not want people to view grace as divine indulgence to sin. They are fearful that the new (and old) Christian will not refrain from sin so they maintain that if the 'Christian' commits sin that he can fall from grace, i.e., loose his salvation. They would keep the Christian fearful of loosing his/her salvation and thus make them to walk the 'straight and narrow'. This is a totally unscriptural position for the sole purpose to keep the Christian fearful. This view does not understand the power of the Holy Spirit within the believer, nor the effectiveness of Gods discipline (Hebrews 12:5-13), nor Gods consequence for when we do sin after becoming a Christian. There is no Scriptural basis for loosing salvation once being made a 'new creation' in Christ (2 Corinthians 5:17). Gods gifts (salvation—eternal life) are irrevocable (Romans 11:29). When we confess Christ as our savior all our sins are forgiven, past, present, and future. John 5:24 states: *"I tell you the truth, whoever hears my word and believes him who sent me has* ***eternal life*** *and will not be condemned; he has crossed over from* ***death to life.****" Emphasis mine.* I do not know how this could be more plain! There is no Scriptural basis for any other position.

Therefore, for the Christian, the Bema Seat Judgment does not address salvation, or our sins; it only judges what we have done in obedient service to Christ in the good works that he had purposed for us to do. For those who just wanted to escape hell and gain heaven but were not interested in an obedient life before Christ, the Bema Seat judgment will be a time of loss of reward that could have been earned by living and doing the will of God while on earth. I think every Christian will receive some reward, but some a great deal more than others.

The Bema Seat Judgment is explained in more detail by the Apostle Paul in 1 Corinthians 3:10-15.

> *By the grace God has given me, I laid a foundation as an expert builder, and someone else is building on it. But each one should be careful how he builds. For no one can lay any foundation other than the one already laid, which is Jesus Christ. If any man builds on this foundation using gold, silver, costly stones, wood, hay or straw, his work will be shown for what it is, because the Day* [Bema Seat Judgment day] *will bring it to light. It will be revealed with fire, and the fire will test the quality of each man's work. If what he has built survives, he will receive his reward. If it is burned up, he will suffer loss; he himself will be saved, but only as one escaping through the flames.*

In this passage, we see that it is our "works" which will be tested. We can recall what Jesus said as recorded in John 15:5: *"I am the vine; you are the branches. If a man remains in me and I in him, he will bear much fruit; apart from me you can do nothing."*

As I have already quoted, 1 Corinthians 13:1-3 describes me if I try to do things "my way". Doing things as I want does not give me the love needed for works pleasing to God. This love, or agape love, comes only from the Holy Spirit, which produces this love within me. If I do not abide in Christ, this love is not produced in me and without Christ I can do nothing—nothing that is acceptable to God. People on earth might be impressed with what I do—but God will not be impressed, and he is the one who is doing the judging.

Things that are done in obedience to Christ are the gold, silver, and precious stones. Things that are done that are sinful or not done because of Christ amount to wood, hay, and stubble. Using the analogy, work may be done in the best of mahogany that is sanded and polished—but when fire is applied, it will burn up. Even things done that are gold, silver, and precious stones will be purified by fire. No sin whatever will enter heaven. *"Nothing impure will ever enter it* [heaven], *nor will anyone who does what is shameful or deceitful, but only those whose names are written in the Lamb's book of life"* (Revelation 21:27).

Many things will be burnt up for no reward. I may be watching television or playing Sunday morning golf instead of—you get the point. I am not saying that you have to be in church every time the doors are open. We love to say that God has a plan and a purpose for our lives—which is absolutely true. If we earnestly seek and follow that plan and purpose in obedient service, Christ will pay or reward that work at the Bema Seat. Do not let this become a burden to keep you from enjoying golf or television— all things have been given for us to enjoy— but do earnestly seek to be about God's will for your life.

Look at it this way. If I did all the things that Christ had for me to do in his plan and purpose for me—I would get 100% of the reward that he had planned for me. Christ makes it worth our while to serve him in this world. You do not have to be obedient to Christ, because he does not force you—but there is a consequence to indifference, which will come to light at the Bema Seat. Eternal life is not lost, nor is it in question, but works will be tested. If you had no works, you would have no reward. I do think that all Christians will have some works, which will be commended and rewarded. But there will be those who have lived faithful and obedient lives who will have a great reward, which they will take with them into heaven.

The Christian has at least three things going for him/her. First, we receive the free gift of eternal life. Do not go past this gift so fast—think about it, as to how great it is. How much would you spend if you needed to 'buy' your eternal life? Second, Christians have an inheritance in Christ—just for being God's children (Romans 8:16-17). Third, we have the possibility of a great reward, and to hear the words from Christ himself, "Well done, good and faithful servant" (Matthew 25:21).There will not be the sin of envy in heaven, but I am sure we will be able to plainly see those who have dedicated their lives to obedient service to Christ and those who have not. It will be a visual thing. I do not know just how this will be, but, for example, if you see me in my military uniform, you would be able to see that I have the United States Air Force "Distinguished Flying Cross." We will see Christ in all of his glory when we meet him in heaven, and we are promised to be glorified along with him. So do not take lightly his instructions for us now—and fight the good fight, along with the Apostle Paul and countless others.

When will the Bema Seat Judgment take place? The Bema Seat Judgment will take place after Christ returns for the church, which will end the church age or the age of grace. Revelation 22:12 records Jesus as saying, *"Behold, I am coming soon! My reward is with me, and I will give to everyone according to what he has done."*

It has been nearly two thousand years since Christ spoke these words to John. I think a better translation would have been—'when I come, I will come quickly.' When Christ comes for us, things will happen very fast—in the twinkling of an eye!

The last seven years, which we call the tribulation, do not necessarily start immediately after the removal of the Church; there could possibly be months or years between the two events. Scripture does not address this.

~ *The Great White Throne* ~

At the end of the tribulation, Christ establishes his one thousand year reign on earth. During the one thousand years, Satan is bound, so that he cannot deceive the nations during that time (Revelation 20:1-3). At the end of the one thousand year reign of Christ, Satan is released for a short period of time to deceive the nations—one final time. Satan is then caught up and thrown directly into the Lake of Fire (Revelation 20:7-10). Earth and sky pass away, and a Great White Throne is established. At this time, all unbelievers are gathered for judgment. The works of the unbelievers are ungodly sins and are judged in order to assign punishment for those sins. These events are recorded for us in Revelation 20:1-15.

Revelation 20: 1-3:

> *And I saw an angel coming down out of heaven, having the key to the Abyss and holding in his hand a great chain. He seized the dragon, that ancient serpent, who is the devil, or Satan, and bound him for a thousand years. He threw him into the Abyss, and locked and sealed it over him, to keep him from deceiving the nations anymore until the thousand years were ended. After that, he must be set free for a short time.*

Verses 7-15:

> *When the thousand years are over, Satan will be released from his prison and will go out to deceive the nations in the four corners of the earth—Gog and Magog—to gather them for battle. In number they are like the sand on the seashore. They marched across the breadth of the earth and surrounded the camp of God's people, the city he loves. But fire came down from heaven and devoured them. And the devil, who deceived them, was thrown into the lake of burning sulfur, where the beast and the false prophet had been thrown* (a thousand years earlier). *They will be tormented day and night forever and ever. Then I saw a great white throne and him who was seated on it. Earth and sky fled from his presence, and there was no place for them. And I saw the dead, great and small, standing before the throne, and books were opened. Another book was opened, which is the book of life. The dead were judged according to what they had done as recorded in the books. The sea gave up the dead that were in it, and death and Hades gave up the dead that were in them, and each person was judged according to what he had done. Then death and Hades were thrown into the lake of fire. The lake of fire is the second death. If anyone's name was not found written in the book of life, he was thrown into the lake of fire.*

There will be degrees of punishment for the ungodly, even as there are degrees of reward for the believer. No one at the Great White Throne judgment has his/her name written in the Lamb's book of life. The book is there and available only to confirm to anyone who may want to check about his/her name that it is, in fact, not in the book. There are probably those who know, without looking, that their name is not there, but I can visualize many 'religious' people who were deceived by false prophets into thinking that "there are many ways to God." (Matthew 7:15-23). Jesus refutes that by saying, *"No one comes to the Father except through me"* (John 14:6b). Part of our work as a Christian is to know the Word of God and to share it with all who will listen—we may well help save someone from this anguish. It is the 'love of Christ' that prompts us to do this.

I do not know how long you have been a Christian, nor am I aware of all the blessed effort for Christ that you have done. I do encourage you to continue in faithful obedience and the joy of fellowship with Christ, until you can no longer work for him. I agree with the Apostle Paul that,

"Therefore we do not lose heart. Though outwardly we are wasting away, yet inwardly we are being renewed day by day. For our light and momentary troubles are achieving for us an eternal glory that far outweighs them all. So we fix our eyes not on what is seen, but on what is unseen. For what is seen is temporary, but what is unseen is eternal" (2 Corinthians 4:16-18).

~ Additional thoughts ~

While it is true that Jesus Christ is the one who is our Judge, there is another type of judgment in which we are involved, as is suggested in the following verse. *"Therefore judge nothing before the appointed time; wait till the Lord comes. He will bring to light what is hidden in darkness and will expose the motives of men's hearts. At that time each will receive his praise from God"* (1 Corinthians 4:5).

The Apostle Paul is speaking of judgments to be made, which have to do with following Christian principles in our daily living. When confronting a young man in Corinth who was living a sexually immoral lifestyle, Paul states in 1 Corinthians 5:12-13: *"What business is it of mine to judge those outside the church? Are you not to judge those inside? God will judge those outside. 'Expel the wicked man from among you.'"*

This is a different kind of judgment than we are talking about after our resurrection. We are to use God's wisdom, in love, in making these kinds of judgments, and we are not to avoid such kind of judgment.

In Matthew 7:1-2 it says: *"Do not judge, or you too will be judged. For in the same way you judge others, you will be judged, and with the measure you use, it will be measured to you."* Christ goes on to say that we must judge ourselves—to remove the 'plank' from our own eye. He calls us hypocrites if we judge others and not first judge ourselves. In John 7:24 Christ cautions us to *"Stop judging by mere appearances, and make a right judgment."* We like to be subjective in our judgments and not objective *(and make a right judgment)* and to use humility, love, wisdom and truth when we judge things. We are to learn to make correct judgments—that is to be carefully consistent with scriptural truth. It is the ungodly sinner who loves to quote Matthew 7:1-2 because he does not want you to make an evaluation concerning his sinful ways, but you are in fact to 'judge all things'. The Apostle Paul tells us in 1 Corinthians 6:2-3 that, *"Do you not know that the saints will judge the world? And if you are to judge the world, are you not competent to judge trivial cases? Do you not know that we will judge angels? How much more the things of this life!"*

We are told not to judge from outward appearances, or in a self-centered way, but we must learn to judge correctly because we will judge the world and we will judge angels—we must learn to make judgments correctly!!

It is not given to us to judge the unbeliever. Christ will do that. Protecting ourselves from the ungodly by military defense, or personal defense, is not judging the ungodly, even if they are killed in the process. Use of capital punishment for deserving crimes is not to be avoided (Genesis 9:5-6). God has given us instructions in this area, and we ignore those instructions only in disobedience to God.

Again, everyone who is condemned by Christ is condemned to "eternal death." God, through the Holy Spirit, "convicts" people of their sin—which is to make them aware that what they are doing is wrong and that they should repent and change. This condemnation by Christ is held until judgment day. John 3:17-18 puts it this way: *"For God did not send his Son into the world to condemn the world, but to save the world through him. Whoever believes in him is not condemned, but whoever does not believe stands condemned already because he has not believed in the name of God's one and only Son."*

Part of our work is to witness by sharing the "good news" that the death, burial, and resurrection of Christ provides for the forgiveness of sins. We must make known the standard of conduct God expects of us. We are not to condemn or be surprised at failure, but seek restoration to holy living. We are not to be the "policeman" for God, though we do set a standard for behavior. We, in not condemning, must still hold as unacceptable some behavior and to help prevent it in our midst. This may even include taking legal action against some for their behavior.

Also, God made Christ our judge for two reasons: first, *"That all may honor the Son just as they honor the Father"* (John 5:23); second, *"And he has given him authority to judge because he is the Son of Man"* (John 5:27). Jesus is the God-man, who is able to judge, knowing all the problems first hand of living in the flesh. No one can say, "But you do not know what it was like to live in the flesh, so you are not fit to be my judge."

In addition, consider the saying "Once saved always saved, no matter what you do". It may be true, but it is more accurate to say, "Once saved always saved, and it does make a difference what you do." What is it about the statement "has crossed over from death to life" that is hard to understand? There are those who think that people can be "given" eternal life and who, by their willful decision, "give it back" and, thereby, "lose" their eternal life. People do not have the power to gain their salvation, nor do they have the power to give it away. Some take Scriptures, such as 1 Corinthians 15:2, as their proof. *"By this gospel you are saved, if you hold firmly to the word I preached to you. Otherwise, you have believed in vain."* This may be a valid point, but I think the answer is found in Hebrews 6:4-9. Verse 9 concludes that even though Paul spoke as he did, he was confident as he stated: " . . . *we are confident of better things in your case—things that accompany salvation."* People can be drawn to God (Verses 4-6) and "believe", yet not have the experience of crossing from death to life. While God is the ultimate judge of this, if God has, in fact, given to us the gift of eternal life, his gifts and his call are irrevocable. (Romans 11:29). I do not see God taking back the best gift that can be given to anyone. The question is whether the person's belief really resulted in salvation or not in the first place. Only God knows. What I do know is *"Whoever believes in him is not condemned, but whoever does not believe stands condemned already because he has not believed in the name of God's one and only son"* (John 3:18). I also believe Romans 8:1-2. *"Therefore, there is now no condemnation for those who are* ***in*** *Christ Jesus, because through Christ Jesus the law of the Spirit of life set me free from the law of sin and death."* Some manuscripts include "who do not live according to the sinful nature but according to the Spirit." This is not in the original and should not be included. Some zealous scribe who wanted to insure people's salvation probably added this phrase.

Christ does not condemn or judge at this time.

As Christians we are placed under God's Grace. We are removed from being under the law. <u>It was the law that condemned us to death</u>. Grace does not condemn us—even if we sin.

~ *The Kingdom* ~

There will be different kinds of people in Christ's millennial Kingdom. First, there will be normal (flesh and blood—like now) people who come from the nations, who were invited into the kingdom after the tribulation. They will have normal, flesh and blood children—with sin natures. It will be the descendents of these people who will rebel when Satan is released to deceive the nations one final time. This demonstrates that even when living in a perfect environment, with perfect government, the sin nature cannot be made acceptable. The sin nature will cause rebellion against God, even when all else is perfect. Second, there will be resurrected people, with resurrected bodies, who do not have sin natures, and who will be ruling and reigning with Christ. Christ will be ruling in person.

~ The Sin Nature ~

The sin nature cannot be rehabilitated—it must be put to death. It can be put to death in only two ways: it can be put to death with Christ on the Cross, or it can be taken with you into the Lake of Fire, which is the second death, and is eternal. The sin nature has never been obedient to God! Our sin nature is always in rebellion to God's will. It is only by our new spiritual nature, as Christians, that we can say 'no' to the sin nature and have victory over our own sin nature.

Chapter 11

~ The Incarnation ~

We need to have a good understanding of Christ's Incarnation and of what Christ did to become human like us, and of his becoming our Redeemer and Savior. I am always impressed when someone expresses an interest about Christ as the God-man, wanting to know what Christ knew and what his capabilities or limitations were as a baby, as a young child, and during his earthly ministry. I have considered those questions, as well. If Christ was fully God and fully man from the beginning of his Incarnation—what are we to understand of him in those early years and during his earthly ministry? How, if Christ had all the powers and attributes of deity, could he really be our example for living, as Peter said in 1 Peter 2:21. *"To this you were called, because Christ suffered for you, leaving you an example, that you should follow in his steps."* This chapter will address these questions, as well as the question of what Christ gave up to become human.

~ Introduction ~

Christ's Incarnation is totally unique. It has happened only once and will never happen again. It was foretold in the Scriptures that Christ would be born as the God-man, the Messiah in human flesh.

> *For to us a child is born, to us a son is given, and the government will be on his shoulders. And he will be called Wonderful Counselor, Mighty God, Everlasting Father, Prince of Peace. Of the increase of his government and peace there will be no end. He will reign on David's throne and over his kingdom, establishing and upholding it with justice and righteousness from that time on and forever. The zeal of the Lord Almighty will accomplish this.* (Isaiah 9:6-7)

The circumstances of the birth of Christ were also foretold in Scriptures. One example is Isaiah 7:14. *"Therefore the Lord himself will give you a sign: The virgin will be with child and will give birth to a son, and will call him Immanuel."* As we know, the translation of Immanuel is "God with us."

Matthew quoted this scripture as being fulfilled by the birth of Jesus. *"All this took place to fulfill what the Lord had said through the prophet* (Isaiah) *'The virgin will be with child and will give birth to a son, and they will call him Immanuel'—which means, 'God with us'"* (Matthew 1:22-23).

The Apostle Paul helped us to understand the dual nature of Jesus Christ. Speaking of the gospel (good news) concerning Christ that he was called to preach, Paul says: "*. . . the gospel he* (God) *promised beforehand through his prophets in the Holy Scriptures regarding his Son, who as to his human nature was a descendant of David* (human—Mary was a descendant of David), *and who through the Spirit of holiness* (the Holy Spirit) *was declared with power to be the Son of God by his resurrection from the dead: Jesus Christ our Lord"* (Romans 1:2-4). Jesus Christ is the God-man. Mary, the young virgin and a physical descendent of King David, was chosen to produce the human part of the God-man. The Holy Spirit provided the additional part for Mary's pregnancy, normally provided by a human father, as well as the spiritual part of this God-man, which was the second person of the God-head, namely Christ.

~ The Son of God ~

The Deity of Jesus Christ, who is called the 'Son of God', is more fully developed in the New Testament Scriptures than in the Old Testament Scriptures, although his deity is addressed in the Old Testament, as well. Psalm 2 speaks of the 'Anointed One' (Christ or Messiah) who was God's Messiah in terms that we understand today. Verse 7 states, *"I will proclaim the decree of the Lord: He said to me* (the Father speaking to Christ), *'You are my Son; today I have become your Father.'"* This, of course, did not happen in the physical sense during the times of the Psalms but occurred physically when the Virgin Mary conceived, by the Holy Spirit (at the direction of the Father), and bore a son—the God-man, Jesus Christ. God the Father did not 'beget' the 'Deity' of Christ, who always existed, but begat the 'flesh' or human part of Christ incarnate. As such, Jesus is the only human being 'beget' by God the Father, and, thus, he is the "only begotten son of God". Spiritually, Christ took the 'position or role' of a faithful son as a member of the God-head in eternity past, and, as such, became a faithful 'Son of God' to 'God the Father'. As an eternal member of the triune God, Christ, the Messiah, has always existed as a co-equal member of the God-head with all the attributes, equally shared, by the God-head.

The Old Testament speaks of Jesus Christ as the 'Son of God' and of his eternal existence. But it is in the New Testament that we have a much better understanding of who Jesus Christ is. For example, the Apostle John in his Gospel establishes Christ's central role in creation, his Incarnation, and his glory.

> *In the beginning was the Word and the Word was with God, and the Word was God. He was with God in the beginning. Through him all things were made* (created): *without him nothing was made that has been made. In him was life, and that life was the light of men. The light shines in the darkness, but the darkness has not understood it."* (John 1:1-5) *"The Word became flesh and made his dwelling among us. We have seen his glory, the glory of the One and Only* (or the Only Begotten), *who came from the Father, full of grace and truth."* (John 1:14)

John tells us that Jesus Christ was the 'Word' that God the Father used when he brought things into being. Christ was the 'spoken word' of God. When the Father spoke, Christ was the power of that 'word' which brought things into being. The Father would speak what he wanted done, and Christ would accomplish the work. Part of God's plan was for the Incarnation of Christ, which is fulfilled by Christ's obedience to God.

John affirms that this 'Word' became flesh (took on human form) to live with mankind, and then, he reaffirms that Christ was still full of the glory of his eternal, spiritual nature. John saw the glory of Jesus Christ, along with Peter and James (John's brother), on the mountain of transfiguration (Matthew 17:2). John was able to write with authority of what he had actually seen: a brief glimpse of Christ's glory, before Christ had died on the cross, had been resurrected, and had received back the glory that he had given up to be made in human form.

~ *Attributes of the Son* ~

It is through the work of the Incarnate Christ that we have eternal life with Christ. In Christ is life. *"For as the Father has life in himself, so he has granted the Son to have life in himself"* (John 5:26). All members of the Godhead (Father, Son, and Holy Spirit) are equal in the attributes of the triune God, but in this Scripture, we see a functional order and authority established within the Godhead. The 'Father' has 'granted' the 'Son' to have life within himself. Christ has taken the role of an obedient Son to the Father. This relationship was established in eternity past. When Christ took upon himself flesh and blood, the role of an obedient Son remained the same. When Christ became the God-man, he maintained the role as the obedient Son of God, but now confined to human flesh as his abode. God did become the father of the 'physical' part of Jesus Christ, making Jesus 'the only begotten son' of God. When Jesus Christ wanted to identify himself with humankind (with flesh and blood), he took upon himself the name 'Son of man.' Christ maintained all the attributes that he had before the incarnation, but subordinated himself and all of his attributes to the complete and total will of the Father. The only thing that Christ gave up to become the God-man was his 'visible glory', which Peter, James, and John glimpsed on the Mountain of Transfiguration. They were allowed to see Christ's natural glory, unsuppressed, for that moment in time. In John 17:5, we see Christ asking the Father to glorify him with the glory he had with the Father before the world began. Christ's glory was restored, and the Father exalted him to the highest place (Philippians 2:9-11, Ephesians 1:19-23). When we see Christ again, we will behold him in all of his power and glory!

The Scriptures do not tell us how Christ maintained all the rest of his attributes, which we could not see except in his behavior, such as his holiness, love, mercy, etc, because he maintained the fullness of the Father at all times. *"For God was pleased to have all his fullness dwell in him, and through him to reconcile to himself all things, whether things on earth or things in heaven, by making peace through his blood, shed on the cross"* (Colossians 1: 19-20). While on earth as the God-man, Christ did not use his own power to do things, or his own omniscience to know things, and was located within a physical body—so could not be omnipresent. Christ did not walk on the water by his own power, but by the same power Peter walked on the water—the power of the Holy Spirit. Christ did not calm the seas by his own power, but by the power of the Holy Spirit. Christ did not 'know' things because of his own omniscience, but only knew things as the Holy Spirit gave him wisdom, understanding, knowledge, etc. Christ limited himself to our level of ability and he became our example of submission and obedience to the Father. Thus, Christ is our example for living the Christian life.

As a baby, Christ was only aware like normal babies. As a very young child, Christ was a normal very young child. However, there was a difference between Christ and all other children (us)—Christ did not have a 'sin nature' to lead him to sin. All the rest of us were conceived with sin natures—which has caused us to be sinful and selfish from conception. As a young boy at the Temple in Jerusalem, Christ was aware of exactly what the Father wanted him to know.

~ The Godhead ~

You can consider this a parenthetical, but at this point; it will be beneficial to understand the different roles of each member of the God-head. Two examples will demonstrate the roles each member of the Godhead has taken. This will help us understand what Christ did when he became incarnate.

In Genesis 1:1, we read, *"In the beginning God created the heavens and the earth."* In John 1:3, we know that it was Christ the 'Word' who made (created) everything that was made, so we know that it was Christ who created the heavens and the earth. We know that Christ is obedient to the Father, so we know that it was the Father who spoke the words to create the heavens and the earth. Genesis 1:2 states, *"Now the earth was formless and empty, darkness was over the surface of the deep, and the Spirit of God* (Holy Spirit) *was hovering over the waters."* The Holy Spirit is now involved in the process to form the earth as it was during the pre-flood days. Christ and the Holy Spirit continued the creation process with all members of the Godhead involved when in Genesis 1:26-27 it says, *"Then God said, 'Let us make man in our image, in our likeness, and let them* (man) *rule over the fish of the sea and the birds of the air, over the livestock, over all the earth, and over all the creatures that move along the ground.'"* The use of the pronoun 'us' refers to the triune God involved in creating man (male and female) in their own image (of holiness). Thus, the Father wanted the heavens and the earth, etc. created. The Son creates the heavens and the earth, and the Holy Spirit helps finish the creative process to its final form.

A second example will complete our understanding. We read in John 3:16, *"For God so loved the world that he gave his one and only Son, that whoever believes in him shall not perish but have eternal life."* The Father wanted the provision of salvation for humankind. Christ was sent to provide salvation, which required Christ to take upon himself flesh and blood (incarnation) in order to die (physically) on the Cross in payment for the sins of the world. After Christ returns to heaven, the Holy Spirit is then sent at 'Pentecost' to apply to humankind the salvation provided by the God-man Christ Jesus. The Holy Spirit works in those who will believe Christ's sacrifice for sins and his provision for salvation, to provide forgiveness and the free gift of eternal life, and to sanctify those who have been given eternal life.

This certainly does not give in total detail the role of each member of the Godhead, but it gives a brief 'order of authority' within the Godhead. Remember the eternal equality of the members of the Godhead, yet the willing submission of each member to each other as the 'One God of Heaven'.

Our final question to address is, "What did Christ give up when he became human?"

~ *Made Himself Nothing* ~

In Philippians 2:5-8, we read the following.

> *Your attitude should be the same as that of Christ Jesus: Who, being in very nature God, did not consider equality with God something to be grasped, but made himself nothing* (emptied himself)*, taking the very nature of a servant, being made in human likeness. And being found in appearance as a man, he humbled himself and became obedient to death— even death on a cross.*

We need to pay close attention to what takes place in these verses, because we are expected to have the same attitude Christ had, which is to say that we need to do the same thing that he did—at least in the part that we can do in being like him.

First, we want to understand what Christ gave up when he 'made himself nothing' or 'emptied himself', which is directly from the Greek in this passage.

In Christ's high priestly prayer, just before his arrest and crucifixion, he says, *"And now, Father, glorify me in your presence with the glory I had with you before the world began"* (John 17:5). When Christ came to earth for the "Incarnation", he gave up his glory—he received his glory back after his passion on the Cross. Christ remained deity, because he represented the fullness of the Father at all times, even while on earth. It must be understood that Christ was always equal to the Father, while on earth, except for the glory of God for us to behold or see. Because he had given up his glory, while on earth, he asked his Father if he would give him back his glory after the Cross. It was granted, and the second time that Christ comes to earth, it will be in power and 'great glory'. *"When the Son of Man comes in his glory, and all the angels with him, he will sit on his throne in heavenly glory"* (Matthew 25:31). We can understand his glory as the visual display of power and splendor, and majesty, and deity. It was this visual display that Christ gave up to be the God-man on earth. Everything else was present, but was restrained or subdued in order to carry out the will of the Father.

It is difficult, if not impossible, for us to understand or comprehend how Christ could restrain and subdue the attributes of his Deity, such as his omniscience, omnipotence, etc., to know or be aware or to do only what the Father wanted him to know, or to be aware of or to do. Yet this is exactly what Scripture tells us using Christ's own words. While we do not comprehend this, we must accept and believe Christ's own words to us. Let us see what is said and what happened.

~ The Incarnate Christ ~

When Jesus, as the God-Man, was born of the Virgin Mary, he was in every way a human baby, with the only exception that he did not have a 'sin nature', because God was his 'spiritual and physical' father. This is exactly the same spiritual way Adam and Eve were created. Christ was able to be tempted, because he was in the 'flesh', but having no sin nature, he did not sin. As a baby, Jesus knew no more that any other baby, because his attributes of Deity were completely subdued, even though he still represented the 'fullness of God.' (Colossians 1:19)

The only knowledge of Jesus' development in childhood is found in Luke 2: 41-52. This concerns the episode when Jesus was twelve years old and his family had taken him from Nazareth to Jerusalem, as was their custom for the Feast of the Passover. On their return trip home, his family missed him and returned to Jerusalem to find him. It took them three days to find him. *". . . they found him in the temple courts, sitting among the teachers, listening to them and asking them questions. Everyone who heard him was amazed at his understanding and his answers"* (46-47). It can be said at that time that Jesus knew God was his "Father". *"'Why were you searching for me?' he asked. Didn't you know I had to be in my Father's house?'"* (49). Luke goes on to write, *"And Jesus grew in wisdom and stature, and in favor with God and men"* (52). From Luke, we can only conclude that Jesus grew in wisdom and stature during his childhood, that by age twelve he had significant insight as to whom he was, and that he knew God was his 'father'. What more we wish to learn about Jesus as the Incarnate Christ, we will learn from Jesus' own words concerning himself.

In the Gospel of John, we have Jesus' reply to the Jews who were persecuting him because he was not only healing people on the Sabbath but also claiming to be equal to God, a reply that clearly denotes Jesus' understanding of his position as God-man.

> *Jesus gave them this answer: "I tell you the truth, the Son can do nothing by himself; he can do only what he sees his Father doing, because whatever the Father does the Son also does. For the Father loves the Son and shows him all he does. Yes, to your amazement he will show him even greater things than these"* (John 5: 19-20). *"By myself I can do nothing; I judge only as I hear, and my judgment is just, for I seek not to please myself but him who sent me"* (30).

Of course, Christ can do things—he is the one who created all things. *"For by him all things were created: things in heaven and on earth, visible and invisible, whether thrones or powers or rulers or authorities; all things were created by him and for him"* (Colossians 1:16). All this creation happened before the Incarnation. Christ is all powerful and can do things; it is that Christ, as the God-man on earth, did not do anything on his own—he totally submitted himself to do nothing except what the Father wills. *"For I have come down from heaven not to do my will but to do the will of him who sent me"* (John 6:38).

Jesus goes on to say that eventually the Jews would know who he really is. *"When you have lifted up the Son of Man, then you will know that I am the one I claim to be and that I do nothing on my own but speak just what the Father has taught me"* (John 8:28). This reinforces the knowledge of Jesus' human condition. He learns from and follows his Father, God. In further evidence of his submission to God, while on earth, Jesus says the following about his return to earth: *"No one knows about that day or hour, not even the angels in heaven, nor the Son, but only the Father"* (Matthew 24:36; Mark 13:32). Christ is an all-knowing member of the Godhead, but while on earth, Christ limited his knowledge and awareness and power to what the Father was pleased for him to know and be aware of and to be able to do.

From what Christ said about himself, while on earth, we must conclude that his total purpose was to do the will of the Father; that he did only what the Father reveled to him, or instructed him; that by himself he could do nothing but only speak what the Father taught him; and that his knowledge was limited to what the Father reveled to him. This may be hard for us to understand—but this is exactly what Christ said of himself. *"I have come to do your will, O God"* (Hebrews 10:7b). *"Then he said, 'Here I am, I have come to do your will'"* (9).

Even in the Garden of Gethsemane when Christ was struggling with the immensity of the Cross ahead of him, *"My soul is overwhelmed with sorrow to the point of death"* (Matthew 26:38) and he was seeking if there was any other way to accomplish the will of the Father, he still was true to the Father's will. *"My Father, if it is possible, may this cup be taken from me. Yet not as I will, but as you will"* (Matthew 26:39b). It is always to the plan of the Father that Christ was totally dedicated. John 3:16 illustrates this. It was the Father who so loved the world that he sent his only begotten Son. Of course, the Son and the Holy Spirit love the world as well, but it was the Father's plan to send the Son. It was the Father's plan (Genesis 1:26) when he said, *"Let us make man in our image, in our likeness . . ."* Jesus made it plain that he was not doing "his own thing" but that he was doing the Father's will. Jesus limited himself, in everything, to do only what the Father wanted him to do. Jesus limited himself so that he could do nothing except what the Father showed or approved or directed. Jesus' purpose was to please the Father and be obedient to the Father and to limit his own knowledge, i.e., in not knowing the day or hour of his return in glory. I am sure that Christ, in heaven, now knows this information, but while on earth, before the Cross, he did not. The conclusion must be made that from birth, while Jesus was still God, that he had voluntarily limited his knowledge, his awareness, his development, his power, to be totally obedient and dependent on the will and plan and provision of the Father. We need to understand that Jesus' development from a baby on was at the discretion of the Father as to what Jesus knew, understood, and was aware of and was physically able to do. This was in accordance with the will of the Father. We are not aware of the growth process of Jesus as to all that he knew and when he knew it, but only that it was at the discretion of the Father in Heaven. As we have seen, there were even things that Jesus was not aware of, even as an adult in his earthly ministry. The submission of Christ to the Father was unique in the Incarnation, but Christ's total submission to the Father was not. Christ, from the very beginning of all things, had submitted himself to God the Father. The Holy Spirit subordinates himself to both the Father and the Son and proceeds from both the Father and the Son in obedience to them (John 15:26). This is true even though there is total equality within the Godhead.

When Christ accepted hardship, isolation, ill-treatment, malice, and misunderstanding, and finally, death on a cross—he suffered. He has instructed us to pick up our cross and follow him—that means that we too will suffer for being a Christian—this is just the way the Father planned it. I do not ask for suffering—but I know it will be part of my life, just as it was part of Christ's life. Hebrews 11, the faith chapter of the Scriptures, describes how faithful people have suffered throughout human history.

Hebrews 12:1-12 gives us instruction about suffering.

> *Therefore, since we are surrounded by such a great cloud of witnesses, let us throw off everything that hinders and the sin that so easily entangles, and let us run with perseverance the race marked out for us. Let us fix our eyes on Jesus, the author and perfecter of our faith, who for the joy set before him endured the cross, scorning its shame, and sat down at the right hand of the throne of God. Consider him who endured such opposition from sinful men, so that you will not grow weary and lose heart.*

> *In your struggle against sin, you have not yet resisted to the point of shedding your blood. And you have forgotten that word of encouragement that addresses you as sons* [Children]:
>
> *"My son, do not make light of the*
> *Lord's discipline,*
> *and do not lose heart when he*
> *rebukes you,*
> *because the Lord disciplines those he*
> *loves,*
> *and he punishes everyone he accepts*
> *as a son* [child].
>
> *Endure hardship as discipline; God is treating you as sons. For what son is not disciplined by his father? If you are not disciplined (and everyone undergoes discipline), then you are illegitimate children and not true sons. Moreover, we have all had human fathers who disciplined us and we respected them for it. How much more should we submit to the Father of our spirits and live! Our fathers disciplined us for a little while as they thought best; but God disciplines us for our good, that we may share in his holiness. No discipline seems pleasant at the time, but painful. Later on, however, it produces a harvest of righteousness and peace for those who have been trained by it.*
>
> *Therefore, strengthen your feeble arms and weak knees. "Make level paths for your feet," so that the lame may not be disabled, but rather healed."* (Emphasis mine).

As correctly observed—there are too few who call themselves Christians who are really serious about living an obedient, disciplined, loving, grace—filled life in submissive obedience to the Father. Christ was truly our example.

Paul continues in his instructions with this warning against refusing God.

> *Make every effort to live in peace with all men and to be holy; without holiness no one will see the Lord. See to it that no one misses the grace of God and that no bitter root grows up to cause trouble and defile many. See that no one is sexually immoral, or is godless like Esau, who for a single meal sold his inheritance rights as the*

oldest son. Afterward, as you know, when he wanted to inherit this blessing, he was rejected. He could bring about no change of mind, though he sought the blessing with tears." (Hebrews 12:14-1)

For the Christians who want joy and peace and God's blessing in their lives, there is no option about obedience and holiness and submission to the will of God. The lack among Christians of these very things is the reason that so few Christians experience joy and peace and God's blessing in their lives.

A lack of understanding of the Incarnation has caused many problems that are present in all other religions of the world. People who have problems understanding the virgin birth, sacrificial atonement, the resurrection, the miracles of Christ and the Apostles—the feeding of the thousands—the walking on water, the raising of the dead, etc, generally stem from a poor understanding of the incarnation of Christ. It is here that Jews, Muslims, Unitarians, Jehovah's Witnesses, and Mormons, along with others who travel the 'wide way of just being religious' stumble and fall. When it is understood and accepted that Jesus is both divine and human, all the problems associated with the Scriptures melt away.

Paul, in Romans 1:1-4, gives the testimony.

Paul, a servant of Christ Jesus, called to be an apostle and set apart for the gospel of God—the gospel he promised beforehand through his prophets in the Holy Scriptures regarding his Son, who as to his human nature was a descendant of David, and who through the Spirit of holiness was declared with power to be the Son of God by his resurrection from the dead: Jesus Christ our Lord."

The resurrection of Jesus Christ was well documented as Paul outlined in his letter to the Corinthians. (1 Corinthians 15:3-8). We must accept this testimony as true. The Holy Spirit will give to the believer an internal testimony that the Scriptures are true. Unbelievers will always find trouble with these facts and, therefore, deny the resurrection and, consequently, the Incarnation of the Son of God.

Our attitude of total submission to the Father, and the Son, and the Holy Spirit should be a given for each of us and may our Heavenly Father bless us with his presence in our life.

The Messiah who emptied himself for us has now been placed above everything, in this present age and also in the age to come. (Ephesians

1:19-23) Let us bow our knees before him now—in submission. Everyone will eventually bow before him. *"Therefore God exalted him to the highest place and gave him the name that is above every name, that at the name of Jesus every knee should bow, in heaven and on earth and under the earth, and every tongue confess that Jesus Christ is **Lord,** to the glory of God the Father"* (Philippians 2:9-11). (Emphasis mine). This reminds me of an old advertisement slogan which said, "You can pay me now, or you can pay me later".

Chapter 12

~ What is the Real Christmas Gift? ~

We celebrate the physical birth of Christ Jesus into the world of humanity every year. Christ, the Messiah, was God's gift to humankind in a very special way.

In order for God's gift to humanity to happen, Christ, the second person of the Godhead, who is very God, with all the attributes, along with the Father and the Holy Spirit, of being eternally wise, totally powerful, clothed in righteousness and honor and glory—the epitome of holiness—had to empty himself of all his glory and honor to be made a human being—like us. (Philippians 2:5—8)

In regard to becoming a human being, Hebrews 2:7, quoting Psalm 8, says, *"You made him a little lower than the angels; . . ."* We ask ourselves, "How in the world should Christ ever be considered to have been made a little lower that the angels?" Christ, with all the attributes of deity, now made a little lower than the angels? The fact is that Christ did not give up all of his attributes—though he did not use them while on earth. Christ did set aside his rightful glory that surrounded him in heaven. Christ did not give up his deity, but he did set aside his use of his omnipotence, omniscience, omnipresence, and made himself totally dependent upon the Father and the Holy Spirit to provide only what he needed at any moment to do the will of the Father while on his earthly mission. Christ became a 'little lower than the angels' in that he now had a physical body that was subject to physical death. Angels are spiritual beings and do not suffer physical death. Angels do not die in the way we classically think of death. The Hebrew understanding of death is that of being separated. Physical death separates us from the physical world. Spiritual death separates us from God, who is the essence of spiritual life. The fallen (evil) angels will be separated from God—which does not mean they will cease to exist, but they will exist apart from the loving God of heaven in a place that we know of as 'eternal hell.'

Christ limited himself to knowing only what a newborn baby knows, when he was born. Jesus was limited every year of his life to knowing only what the Father wanted him to know at that stage of his life. Jesus only knew what a twelve-year-old boy would know, along with any wisdom and understanding that the Father gave him to know at that point of his life. Because Jesus, the human, was also in Spirit, God, and even though limited, yet he was totally obedient to the Father. Jesus was different from us in that he did not have a 'sin nature' from conception like the rest of us received from Adam. This is because Jesus did not have a human father, through which Adam has caused 'many' to become sinners (Romans 5:19), that is the passing of the sin nature on to every descendent of Adam through conception between a 'man' and a woman. God was the 'father' of Jesus through the power of the Holy Spirit. This is why the 'virgin birth' of Jesus is so important.

Christ was never spiritually inferior to angels in any way, but he was now subject to physical pain and suffering and all the other things associated with having a physical, earthly, body. Jesus was subject to such things as being hungry and thirsty, being tired, suffering physical pain, and having all the physical drives that we as human beings experience. Christ took upon himself a physical body, so that he could suffer on the cross as the 'Lamb of God' who would die for the sins of the world.

We should note that Christ limited himself and became totally dependent upon the Father in order to be our example for the way we are to live. As Christ lived totally dependent upon the Father for everything, we, too, are totally dependent upon our Heavenly Father for everything that we need in order to live obediently before Him.

To review: Christ was like us physically—he was unlike us spiritually. Romans 1:2b-4 says, " . . . *who as to his human nature was a descendant of David, and who through the Spirit of holiness was declared with power to be the Son of God by his resurrection from the dead: Jesus Christ our Lord.* " Physically, Christ was human like we are. Spiritually, he was God—without a sin nature that humankind inherited from Adam—who got his sin nature from Satan. Christ explained it to the Pharisees this way in John 8:42-44.

> *If God were your Father, you would love me, for I came from God and now am here. I have not come on my own; but he sent me. Why is my language not clear to you?* (Which is to say—why can you not understand me?) *Because you are unable to hear what I say. You belong to your father, the devil* (spiritually, not physically), *and you want to carry out your father's desire. He was a murderer* (They wanted to murder Jesus, too.) *from the beginning, not holding to the truth, for there is no truth in him. When he lies, he speaks his native language, for he is a liar and the father of lies.*

Jesus Christ was the begotten Son of God in the physical sense, when God became his father, but in the spiritual sense, Christ was not 'created', as such, but took upon himself the role of an obedient Son in the Godhead. (In his book *The Shack*, William Paul Young (no relation to the author) says that there is no chain of authority in the Godhead. That is absolutely not true! There is a chain of authority that goes from the Father to the Son to the Holy Spirit to all of humanity. Authority goes from Christ who is over all mankind—with no exceptions).

What Christ gave up when he became human was his rightful glory and honor that he had always had as the second person of the Godhead from all eternity past. It was this glory that Christ asked the Father to give back to him, as we read in John 17: 4-5. *"I have brought you glory on earth by completing the work you gave me to do. And now, Father, glorify me in your presence with the glory I had with you before the world began."* This is exactly what the Father did, as we read in Philippians 2:9-11. *"Therefore God exalted him to the highest place and gave him the name that is above every name, that at the name of Jesus every knee should bow, in heaven and on earth and under the earth, and every tongue confess that Jesus Christ is Lord, to the glory of God the Father."*

Jesus Christ is using this authority he has, when he gave the command to spread his Word to others. We read in Matthew 28:18-20. *"Then Jesus came to them and said, 'All authority in heaven and on earth has been given to me. Therefore go and make disciple of all nations, baptizing them in the name of the Father and of the Son and of the Holy Spirit, and teaching them to obey everything I have commanded you. And surely I am with you always, to the very end of the age.'"* This applies to us today, because the command extended to his people all the way to the end of this present age—and we are not to the end of this present age yet! You may not be the one baptizing people into the family of God, but you are to teach those in the family of God to obey everything that Christ commanded us to do. Christ will be with us in this effort to the very end of the age.

God's gift to the world did not stop with a baby in a cradle. God's gift to us included a cradle, a cross, and a crown. We have seen the baby of the cradle grow in grace, totally obedient to his Father in heaven, and become our sacrifice as the 'Lamb of God' on the Cross of Calvary. It does not stop there! We will, in the future, see this 'Lamb of God' return as the 'Lion of the tribe of Judah' wearing the diadem Crowns of Heaven, with all of his angels and all the redeemed, to set up the 'Government that shall be upon his shoulders' for all eternity. Every knee will bow before him and confess that he is God. Even those who have hated him, on earth and in heaven, will make that confession of 'Truth', though it will not benefit the lost at that point, for they shall, forever, be condemned to separation from God to exist in hell.

Only a very few people witnessed and visually celebrated God's gift of the Messiah to earth, the most important thing that has ever happened on earth or ever will happen on earth. There were a few shepherds and a few wise men (representing Gentiles) who witnessed Christ's birth or visited the young baby. That's it!! Probably less than fifteen people, other than the immediate family.

Those conspicuously absent from any notification or involvement in this celebration were government leaders, kings, priests, including the High Priest, business men, real estate planners, and other financial advisors. Yes, and there were no 'commoners—like you and me!' Why??

The reason is that God did not want his gift to earth to be killed immediately!! Christ was to be killed—but that was to come later. We read in the Scriptures how the king and the government leaders tried, unsuccessfully, to kill him immediately after his birth. The High Priest, along with the Pharisees, finally did succeed in killing Christ, and among the crowd that cried "crucify him", were the real estate planners, financial advisors, and some of our neighbors, who just flat-out surprised us.

The world did not want God's gift to mankind then, and the world does not want God's gift today, either. Government leaders today would kill him if they could. Our school system has done much to kill what Christ would teach us. Too many of our church leaders ignore him and would be happy if he were dead. Too many of our neighbors are greeting us with 'Happy Holidays', because they, too, would just as soon that Christ was out of the picture. The world did not want Christ then, and the world does not want Christ today!

But, what the world wants does not make a difference—God has given us a King who will soon return and fulfill totally the gift that God has given to the world. If we are to be 'wise men', we will bow upon our knees, even now, and confess that Jesus is Lord—to the glory of God the Father.

A baby in a cradle is cute and sweet and makes little demands on us. But keep in mind, even now, that that baby has grown up, was crucified for our sins, was resurrected from the dead and is now only waiting for the moment when the Father will tell him to return as King of kings and Lord of lords, to judge the world, to judge each of us according to how we have lived for him, and to set up his eternal government to rule and reign forever. I, for one, am on my knees confessing that Jesus is Lord—to the glory of the Father and to my own eternal well-being. As Christ is my Lord I am learning to live the obedient life (John 14:15, 21, 23). May each of you accept this marvelous gift of salvation given to the world through the 'Son of Man', Jesus Christ, and live the spiritual life for which you are intended.

Chapter 13

~ The Philosophies ~

The philosophies, or as we would now call them philosophers, of the 1700's based their thinking on rational human reasoning or on empiricism, which is the practice of relying only on observations and experiments, especially as in the natural sciences. They rejected established understanding of human behavior and motivation, because they rejected revealed knowledge or revelation from God. While common thought included the acceptance of "good and evil" in mankind as revealed from God, the philosophers of the 1700's refused to accept such a premise. Corruption within the 'church' (read wolves in sheep's clothing, Matthew 7:15-20) caused the philosophies to ridiculed the church and rejected the truth, along with everything else the church at the time professed.

One can understand the rejection of pompous, irritating, harsh, and corrupt 'religious' imitators of godliness by the 'run of the mill' individual, but in this case we are 'supposedly' addressing the 'learned thinkers' of the age, who should have been able to look past the corrupt and find the 'truth' contained in the Scriptures. However, it appears that even though they had professed themselves 'wise', they were, in fact, only 'another of the same kind'. They espoused the premise that there was no such thing as sin or evil. Yet every one of them struggled to explain evil in human behavior while denying that it even existed. Those who did acknowledge the existence of personal corruption were not able to accept or understand its source and would blame society itself. They rejected the supernatural, and, thus, rejected a moral God who proclaimed that "good and evil" existed and that man was his own source of evil (read corruption).

Consequently, the philosopher of the 1700's proposed humanist principles to be used to administer civil affairs. A few accepted Deism, as a necessity, but would not accept a Creator who was actively involved in his creation. Their subjective rejection of the true spiritual nature of human beings, even in their own experience, doomed to failure their proposed utopian, humanist societies. They could not comprehend that man, including themselves, could not respond to reason, even sound reason, because all were basically evil. The subjective rejection of the basic sinfulness and depravity of humanity and the naive notion that humans would respond positively to "rational reason" has been demonstrated in the failure of one humanistic society after another. Additionally, the personal lives of humanistic philosophers reflect their own inability to behave in what they would consider "rational behavior".

James, the half-brother of Jesus, in writing to the twelve tribes scattered among the nations, wrote:

> *Who is wise and understanding among you? Let him show it by his good life, by deeds done in humility that comes from wisdom. But if you harbor bitter envy and selfish ambition in your hearts, do not boast about it or deny the truth. Such 'wisdom' does not come down from heaven but is earthly, unspiritual, of the devil. For where you have envy and selfish ambition, there you find disorder and every evil practice. But the wisdom that comes from heaven is first of all pure; then peace-loving, considerate, submissive, full of mercy and good fruit, impartial and sincere.* (James 3:13-17 NIV).

This passage of Scripture shows there are two kinds of 'wisdoms': earthly wisdom and heavenly wisdom. Disorder and every kind of evil practice develop from earthly wisdom and the opposite from heavenly wisdom. When this understanding is applied to human affairs, we can determine by simple observation the source of the "wisdom" that is being used. Every evil practice includes strife and contention and violence, along with other human vices. This, unfortunately, is even found within the "professed" church today as well as in the 1700's and within civil governments. I use the term 'professed church' for those who would claim 'Christianity' as their 'religious persuasion' but by practical observation do not, in fact, base their lives and behavior on Scriptural principles. These leaders want to be thought of as godly and religious but are instead 'just doing their own thing'. Christ addressed this kind of 'religion' with his disciples when he told them, *"Watch out for false prophets. They come to you in sheep's clothing* (religious garb and even priestly robes), *but inwardly they are ferocious wolves. By their fruit you will recognize them"* (Matthew 7:15-16). In these simple words, Christ confirms not only the existence of evil presenting itself within religious clothing, but also we should be able to easily recognize evil behavior by simple observation.

For philosophers to be surprised to find those who operate within the various religions causing disorder and evil practices, only demonstrates their real lack of understanding and their real lack of sound human reasoning and rational observation. It is the denial that anything is "evil" that precludes the recognition of evil. This results with the insistence that there are no absolutes truths and that everything is relative and that there is no right or wrong behaviors. This is a popular philosophical position today, which causes human grief now, even as it did in the 1700's.

Traditionally, philosophy is the study of logic, the basic principles of science, metaphysics, ethics, and aesthetics. In a wider sense, the general principles of any subject can be called its philosophy. Approaching a misuse of the word, as in "my philosophy of life", only indicates individual preference seems to be the way the philosophies used the term. They did not come up with any new or revealing knowledge or wisdom; they only expounded the way they thought things ought to be. Philosophizing then becomes personalizing, which varies only in degree.

The common element in all generalizations (personalizing) is a claim to arrive at knowledge. The real question in philosophy is, "How is knowledge possible?" Attempts to justify knowledge are called epistemology. Then the question "What do you know" demands the next question, "How do you know?" Epistemology becomes the basis of philosophy (knowledge).

There are two general types of epistemology used by the philosophies. The first is empiricism. Empiricism limits all knowledge to that which is based on physical experience or received through the senses. This excludes any revelation of knowledge or developing a theory of behavior on revelation, though a few did allow for some non-sensory aesthetic or religious experience. The second general type of epistemology is best described by rationalism. Rationalism differs from empiricism in that only knowledge derived from the mind itself through reason alone was acceptable. The idea of "innate ideas" as naturally within the mind was claimed. Emmanuel Kant taught that the mind had ideas, but that they were only of value after they were organized.[1]

Within the Western tradition, evil and immorality have been addressed by every philosopher. The source of the evil has been assigned to various things, from society itself to the possession of material wealth.[2] Scriptures assign the source of evil in this world to Satan and the sin nature that dwells within each human soul and spirit.

The involvement of the philosophies in the social changes from the late seventeenth century to today is acknowledged. But it is questioned that better changes could have been instituted if the philosophies had not rejected true Christian wisdom, which left them only to embraced human or earthly "wisdom". It is not argued that corruption and injustice did not exist within monarchies, especially in the Roman Catholic Church and the French Aristocracy. But neither was France the sole problem area in Europe. Improvements in the human condition should have been made in all the countries of Europe. Improvements were already under way through the efforts of godly men through what is known as the Reformation. Martin Luther began the movement to correct the errors of the Catholic Church in 1517 A.D. Sola Scriptura (Scripture only) would have been a good solution for all church and civil corruption. This was reformation with true love and compassion for humanity. It is acknowledged that some "professed Christians" (read wolves in sheep's clothing) created inhumanity, strife, and discord in everything they touched. According to James, this is not wisdom that comes from heaven. It must be concluded that such immoral actions come from "wolves in sheep's clothing" and should not be considered part of Heavenly wisdom. It is found within the "visible church," which includes those who are not part of the "true Church". If the philosophers were truly wise, they would have understood this very simple premise. Their subjective rejection of the supernatural, especially heavenly wisdom that comes from God, and their poor understanding of earthly wisdom as well as pagan (Satanic) religions, caused them to fail miserably. Professing themselves to be wise, they, instead, were totally earthly in their own wisdom, which results in strife, envy and every evil practice.

People who believed in the validity of Christian principles based the United States' Declaration of Independence and the Constitution on those Christian principles. Modern revisionists are trying to rewrite our history and make us a 'humanistic nation' like those created by the philosophies. If this actually occurs, a modern bloody 'French Revolution' can very easily happen in America. Denying the basis of the foundation of the United States would be to step backward into the 'gentle human kindness' and humanistic values and worldly wisdom observed so well in the old USSR.

Within Western thought, there are these two basic philosophical positions, so it should be expected that strife and envy and every evil practice will continue. While Christianity has been the single greatest source for philosophical thought in the Western world, it has never been the only or pure form used for all civil governments or in recent years to maintain those governments. Therefore, it must be noted that Christianity has become less influential in recent years. The most appealing and popular philosophical thought today follows the ancient Greek tradition which seeks truth through the development of rational thought or even plain pragmatism. The process of rational thought excludes any input from what would be considered a supernatural source and relies totally upon what the physical senses and what the mind can comprehend. This began with the Greeks.

The Greeks had no prophets of truth or scriptures like the Hebrews. Homer, who lived in the eighth century B.C., established what later became for the Greeks their relationships to the various 'gods'. Homer did not intend to create a Greek religion with his great epics, but that is how it turned out for the average Greek of his time. Later Greek thought was not based on mystical accounts.[3]

For the later Greeks, mythical religion did give way to a greater reliance on reason and logical thinking. While we classically think of the Greek myths dominating Greek thought, the great Greek thinkers soon depended on rationalism. They saw human beings as having the capacity for rational thought, with a deep need for freedom, and individual worth. The Greeks did not have official creeds with established doctrines, and their religion was more social than spiritual. But even this religious sense would give way to rational thought.[4]

This history has repeated itself within our experience. Thinking is dependent on rational thought, and religion is more social than spiritual.

The Christian Scriptures declare cultic religions, even the Greek religions above, to have originated through Satan, a fallen angel, who operates in defiance of the Creator God of Heaven. (1 Corinthians 10:19-21). This is to say that behind the physical world of sight and sound exists a vast spiritual world that is involved in a spiritual warfare that pores over into the physical world. (Revelation 12). Revelation about man as given in the Scriptures includes those things which otherwise remain unknown. The Apostle Paul firmly established that this knowledge was given to him by Divine revelation (1 Cor 2:10).

Philosophers of the world are either Christian or humanist. Philosophers of this second group are loosely combined because of the universal agreement between them, which is their rejection of the existence of God, or that of the position of the Deist. This leaves them to their own thoughts, which are limited to their physical experience and, supposed, logical and rational thinking. They have failed to explain why good and evil, sin and morality exists at all for the human race. How does a 'spiritual' condition evolve from the 'physical', or why does this condition not exist in the lower primates or other forms of physical life? Man is different but not because of physical evolution. If the 'spiritual' is denied, how are our 'morals' explained? Even though denied, atheistic and deistic philosophers have grappled with morality and sin in man while rejecting that it even exists. Their conclusions have proved ineffective in solving conflicts or producing utopian societies.

The institution of a form of government that would actually defy God did not begin with Lenin; it began with Karl Heinrich Marx. I shall use Karl Marx, because he is most popularly known. Karl Marx in his earlier life was not an atheist. He was born a Jew but was raised in a "Christian" home. The conversion of his father was the result of 'business convenience'. Karl was baptized in the Orthodox Church and was a faithful church member in his earlier school years. His first work, "The Union of the Faithful with Christ", expressed his faith in the atoning death of Jesus Christ.[5] A complete reversal occurred in his life, and the depth of the reversal is demonstrated in his poem "Oulanem".

> Till I go mad and my heart is utterly changed, see this sword—the Prince of Darkness sold it to me . . .
> While for us both the abyss yawns in darkness you will sink down and I shall follow laughing.
> Whispering in you ears 'Descend, come with me, friend.' . . .
> If there is something which devours,
> I'll leap within it, though I bring the world to ruins—
> The world which bulks between me and the abyss,
> I'll smash it to pieces with my enduring curses.
> I'll throw my arms around its harsh reality.
> Embracing me, the world will dumbly pass away.
> And then sink down to utter nothingness, perished, with no existence: That would be really living.

Karl Marx stated that the devil had sold him a plan for the world. Karl Marx's father believed his son was demon possessed when he wrote the Communist Manifesto. Edgar Marx, the son of Karl Marx, addressed his father in a letter dated March 31, 1854, "My Dear Devil".[6]

Marxism has been widely accepted around the world. Many have hailed Karl Marx among the greatest philosophers. Yet his plan for a "workers paradise" has resulted in an estimated one hundred million deaths by those who implemented his philosophy.

Jean Jacques Rousseau, a French Moralist, converted to Roman Catholicism, and argued that civilization and rationalism had led to the degeneration of mankind. However, his personal inconsistency and lack of understanding of Christianity is painfully obvious. The instability of his own character and the paradoxes of his philosophy should have warned the truly observant individual.[7]

Philosophers who based their thinking on rational human reasoning did not contribute any new or improved life-changing philosophy. They did bring about changes but with the same basic strife, envy, and every evil practice about which James warned. New philosophers will come to be known, but the nature of things will remain the same. In fact, new changes to be proposed, if put into effect, will bring with it great loss of human life. The personal lives of the humanist philosophers were not examples to follow. While I have given only two examples, other examples are numerous and just as tragic.

We would like to think the term 'Homo sapiens' or 'wise and thinking man' was really true. However, we must realize that the genus 'Homo' is only an evolutionary term for man and that for the Christian there are only the 'descendants of Adam'. We know the 'descendants of Adam' are not really smart enough to get along without help from their Creator. When the 'wise and thinking man' thinks he can get along on his own, then he is totally dependent on human wisdom, which is limited to 'earthly wisdom'. This always concludes in every evil practice. If this remains a constant, then we will find that the more things change, the more they stay the same.

Endnotes

1 Perry, Marvin, et al. "Immanuel Kant," *Western Civilization* (Boston: Houghton Mifflin Company, 1992) 506-508.

2 Perry, "Rousseau," 413.

3 Perry, "Homer, Shaper of the Greek Spirit," 51.

4 Perry, "Greek Religion," 52.

5 Hutchings, Noah W. "Karl Marx," *Satan's Kingdom and the Second Coming*, (Oklahoma City: Southwest Radio Church, 1983) 44.

6 Hutchings 45.

7 "Rousseau, Jean Jacques," *Encyclopedia International* (New York: Grolier Incorporated, 1966) 581.

Chapter 14

~ *What Can Be Really Known?* ~

For my last chapter, I am moving from the known into thinking about the unknown, simply because I enjoy my own curiosity of thinking. I invite you to 'think with me'. I will be using Scripture to establish the known, which can easily be accepted as 'gospel', but as I think past what the Scripture states, I shall be in the area of the unknown, and my conclusions are my own.

~ *The Known* ~

God is Spirit. John 4:24: *"God is spirit, and his worshipers must worship in spirit and in truth."*

God the Father does not have a physical body, being completely in spirit form. God the Son (Jesus Christ), who is completely God, was also completely man as well, since his incarnation. Romans 1:3-4. *". . . regarding his Son* [Jesus], *who as to his human nature was a descendant of David* (through Mary), *and who through the Spirit of holiness was declared with power to be the Son of God by his resurrection from the dead: Jesus Christ our Lord."*

Jesus is the Son of God, in two ways. Physically, Jesus' mother was the Virgin Mary. Physically, Mary became pregnant by the will of the Father and through the power of the Holy Spirit. (Matthew 1:18; Luke 1:26-27; 31; 34-35). Jesus, therefore, physically became the 'Son of God'. Spiritually the Godhead chose roles and even though each member of the Godhead is totally equal in all the attributes of the 'one God', a hierarchy was established with the titles 'God the Father, God the Son, and God the Holy Spirit. The 'Son' submitted to the 'Father' (John 14:28; John 8:27-29) and the 'Holy Spirit' submitted to both the 'Father' and the 'Son'. John 15:26. *"When the Counselor* (Holy Spirit) *comes, whom I* (Christ) *will send to you from the Father, the Spirit of truth who goes out from the Father, he will testify about me."* The Holy Spirit is 'sent' by Christ as well as the Father. Christ came to do the will of the Father. Christ has the same attributes of the Father, such as eternity, wisdom, power, etc, but has subordinated himself to the position of an obedient Son to the Father.

God, as spirit, is invisible to the human eye. 1Timothy 1:17: *"Now to the King eternal, immortal, invisible, the only God, be honor and glory for ever and ever. Amen."*

God has elected to remain invisible to the physical creation, but not to the spiritual creation. It is his purpose that those who seek him from the physical creation do so from a position of faith (not by physical sight). Hebrews 11:1-3, 6: *"Now faith is being sure of what we hope for and certain of what we do not see. This is what the ancients were commended for. By faith we understand that the universe was formed at God's command, so that what is seen was not made out of what was visible . . . And without faith it is impossible to please God, because anyone who comes to him must believe that he exists and that he rewards those who earnestly seek him."* Romans 1:20: *"For since the creation of the world God's invisible qualities—his eternal power and divine nature—have been clearly seen, being understood from what has been made, so that men are without excuse."*

There are plenty who stumble and fall because of this—but they do so by their own choice—and that because of their own personal wickedness. (Romans 1:18-19). It is as though God has made it easy for those who do not want to believe to use the excuse that they do not "see" God and, therefore, can justify themselves to not have to believe in God, or have to deal with his holiness and righteousness. These people will perish, because God states, *"The righteous will live by faith"* (Romans 1:17). This is opposed to living by "sight."

~ *Man* ~

Man as originally created was, in God's opinion, very good. Man was created in God's image (Gen 1:27), and all that God had created was stated as being very good (Gen 1:31).

Man was created as body, soul, and spirit. I Thessalonians 5:23. *"May God himself, the God of peace, sanctify you through and through. May your whole spirit, soul and body be kept blameless at the coming of our Lord Jesus Christ."*

Luke 1:46-47. *"And Mary said: 'My soul glorifies the Lord and my spirit rejoices in God my Savior.'"*

Those who refuse to acknowledge the invisible God also refuse to acknowledge the invisible makeup of humankind. If they cannot measure, and weigh, and physically observe—they will refuse to accept. To them, thoughts, which are invisible, are only the result of physical and chemical reactions. It is through this thought process that those who do not want to acknowledge God, or acknowledge the Spirit (the Holy Spirit of God who convicts them of sin, and of righteousness, and of judgment (John 16:8-11)), can claim before the world that they are not aware of anything invisible—even when they know that those who do what they are doing deserve death, they not only continue to do ungodly things but also approve of those who do the same as they. (Romans 1:32).

~ The Physical Body ~

Mankind is most knowledgeable of himself as a physical being. We can physically see ourselves, as well as others. This is not to say that we totally understand the complete makeup and complexity of our physical bodies. Although we do know many things about our physical organization, there is much about ourselves yet to be known. We are aware of our bone structure, muscles, body organs, some of our body chemistry, and some electrical activities of the brain and nerves. We have recently discovered genetic codes that cause certain body developments, and other such similar things. The National Institutes of Health and the Department of Energy have completed a project of unprecedented effort to decipher the genetic material that encodes instructions for the development and functioning of the human body. A person's genome is composed of roughly 3 billion pairs of units, called bases, strung together in a linear sequence. Phase 1 of the $3 billion project was to make a rough map of the entire human genome structure. It is true that we are learning more about our bodies every day, and at a fantastic rate. My point is this: We are most aware of our physical being, yet even of our physical bodies we lack complete knowledge. This is after years, even decades of time, even centuries of 'looking' at our physical selves. The complexity of the human body rivals that of the complexity of the physical world, yet there are those who pronounce themselves wise, and state that all that is visible is the result of blind chance in evolutionary development. We do not know how human DNA communicates all of its information to each body cell—yet we pronounce ourselves wise!

~ *The Soul and Spirit* ~

The soul and spirit make up the invisible part of a person. The spirit and the soul have different functions. The interaction between the soul and spirit is impossible for us to totally separate; however, Christ is able to do this and does, when he separates our thoughts and attitudes. (Hebrews 4:12-13). Basically, our thoughts develop in the realm of the soul, and our attitudes develop within the realm of our spirit. It is the physical senses that give input to the soul, which enables us to function in the physical world. It is through our spirit that we are able to function in the spiritual world, either good or bad. It is from the spirit that we produce our attitude toward God, or not, and then from our attitude come thoughts that either acknowledge God, or not. It is our thoughts and attitudes that God will judge in every human being when he judges the "secrets" of men. (Romans 2:16).

~ *The Mind* ~

The combination of our soul and spirit make up the 'mind' of man. Most of society is aware that we are more than just a physical being. There is awareness even in the secular world that man has an invisible part. This invisible part is contained within the physical boundaries of the body. It is generally considered that the invisible part of man functions within the brain. The secular world calls this invisible part the "mind of man." Secular study of the 'mind' has yielded even less information than the secular study of the physical body. Attempts have been made to understand the 'mental' makeup of humans, as well as animals. This is not to say that there have been no discoveries concerning our 'minds', but because of willful disregard of the manufacturer's handbook, which Christians call the Bible, the secular world is totally ignorant of the critical nature of man's invisible part. If we do not turn to Scripture for our understanding, society is doomed to large blank areas in understanding the human being.

~ *Angels* ~

Angels are spirit beings, as is God. They do not have physical bodies as humans do. Because angels are spirits, they too are eternal beings. Angels do not have the attributes of God, such as being omnipotent, omniscience, omnipresent. Angels are much stronger and more capable than humans at the present time, but those who respond to God in faith and obedience will be glorified to a position higher than the angels. (1 Corinthians 6:3; Hebrews 1:14).

Satan, the Devil, known originally as Lucifer, was an Archangel (leader angel) after the order of the Cherubim, and ministered before God (Ezekiel 28:11-19; Isaiah 14:12-20). It was from this position that pride caused him to sin and to be removed from his exalted position before God. In his rebellion, Satan convinced one-third of the angles to rebel with him. Fallen angels are now called demons. Many demons seek to dwell in human hosts, causing a great deal of harm to the human host because of their being fallen (evil) and they seek to dominate and control their human host. Because angels are spirit beings, they are not visible in the physical world, so most people are not aware that Satan's angels exist or that they are very active in the physical world to cause evil. Angels communicate with humans in the same manner that God communicates with us. This includes written material such as the Scriptures, i.e., Satanic written works from Satan, and the speaking directly to the mind with evil thoughts and desires. While there is power from both, God is omnipotent and Satan and his angels are not.

Angels do not marry, nor are they given in marriage, and when we are resurrected and in heaven neither will we marry, or be given in marriage. (Matthew 22:30; Mark 12:25; Luke 20:35). This, however, does not mean that angels are sexless. Angels in Scripture are always presented in masculine form. When angels are allowed to manifest themselves physically, which they did to Abraham, Joshua, Zechariah, Daniel, Mary, etc., they were always presented in the masculine form. We cannot say more than the Scripture tells us and the Scripture does not tell us that angels are sexless. It is well known that demonic activity in the human race focuses on perverting human sexual activity. Christ himself did not marry, nor was given in marriage—are we to conclude that he was sexless? I do not think so!

Angels, with the approval of God, can manifest themselves in the physical world. (Genesis 18:1-2, 19:1-22; 32:22-30).

Satan and the angels that rebelled went from being righteous to being sinful (unrighteous). Angels 'saw' God in all of his glory, so a lack of 'faith' that god existed was not involved in their rebellion. This is a distinct difference from man, whom God has made 'guilty', except for Adam and Eve, from their very start. Mankind starts from a position of lostness and rebellion, and unless he responds to God 'in faith', will remain in that lost position. It can only be speculated whether God gave Satan and the other rebelling angels a chance or a time to repent—the Scriptures do not address this possibility, but with the circumstance of their rebellion, I would suggest that their condition is irreversible—totally.

Only God is divine. Though angels are spirit and man has a spirit—we are not divine. To be divine is to be a deity or God, with the attributes of God.

Though man is not divine, God's *"divine power has given us everything we need for life and godliness through our knowledge of him who called us by his own glory and goodness. Through these he has given us his very great and precious promises, so that through them you may participate in the divine nature and escape the corruption in the world caused by evil desires"* (2 Peter 1:3-4).

~ *In Christ* ~

If we are 'in Christ', we are new creations. If we are 'in Christ', we *"are all sons of God through faith in Christ Jesus"* Galatians 3:26-28 says, *"You are all sons of God through faith in Christ Jesus, for all of you who were baptized into Christ have clothed yourselves with Christ. There is neither Jew nor Greek, slave nor free, male nor female, for you are all one in Christ Jesus."*

~ *Into the Unknown* ~

Please enjoy 'thinking with me' at this point but do not consider this the 'gospel'.

The limitations of the physical body, which a person experiences, cause limitations to the functions of the soul and spirit. If the physical body is unable to see—the soul and spirit are not able to cause the body to see. If the physical body is unable to hear—the soul and spirit can not cause the body to hear. If a person experiences a debilitating disease, such as Alzheimer's, the soul and spirit are limited, even to the point of just existing in a body suffering a coma. Thoughts and attitudes of the soul and spirit are unable to produce healing or improved capability. As the body ages in a natural way—the soul and spirit do not get feeble. The aches and pains of the aging body will be felt in the soul because of the physical senses of pain, etc., which is transmitted to the soul, but my spirit remains as youthful as ever. I am a young spirit now trapped in an old body! However, it is hard for people not to let pain, etc, which is felt through the soul, not affect their thoughts and attitudes. Yet, when the soul and spirit depart from the body, they are able to see and think and observe independently from the body. In cases of personal testimony, my own father and a close personal friend, both of whom I trusted, told me that their spirit left their body and that they could see themselves lying down on a bed below their soul and spirit. My dad said that he was sick at the time with a high fever; my friend was in heart surgery. My friend said that he could see what was going on in the operating room. While it is hard to say what actually happened, it is very possible that things happened as they were described. While they were out of their bodies, their spirit experienced no pain and could see and hear with no limitations imposed. There will be a time, at physical death, when the soul and spirit depart the body, and if you are a Christian, will then be present with the Lord. (2 Corinthians 5:6-9). In our being present with the Lord and absent from the body, our soul and spirit are not blind or deaf, etc, but are able to see and hear and experience the joy of being present with Christ. If the physical body imposes limitations on the soul and spirit, then it would seem that other things could affect the soul and spirit, as well as the soul and spirit affecting the body. Things, such as joy or depression, heartache, frustration, even pleasurable experiences, have their affect on the soul and spirit, as well as on the body. *"A wife of noble character is her husband's crown, but a disgraceful wife is like decay in his bones"* (Proverbs 12:4). *"A man is praised according to his wisdom, but men with warped minds are despised"* (Proverbs 12:8).

~ A Cause and Effect Relationship? ~

It is the soul and spirit that should be in charge of the body, not the physical appetites or the sin nature. It is our soul and spirit that are truly "us." We should not let the body's physical appetites control what we do.

We are responsible to have a right attitude (spirit), and we are to think acceptable thoughts (soul). It is also possible to understand that the soul and spirit adapt to the body, its chemistry and hormones, etc. This is to say that the soul and spirit are neither male nor female, but adjust to the body in which they are placed, and respond as either male or female, depending on the physical body chemistry or hormones in which it has been placed. This could lead us to understand that our glorified body will have neither male nor female chemistry, depending only on the nature of our glorified body, which at this time we do not know what it will be like. Even though angels in Scripture are described in masculine terms—their spiritual body may not contain any masculine chemistry normally considered with a physical body. The purpose of the physical body, while on earth, is designed for earthly duties, procreation and physical intimacy between husband and wife. It does not necessarily reflect what the glorified body should be when there is neither marrying nor given in marriage in heaven. Our intimacy with God, even now, can and should be closer than that of a husband and wife, and certainly does not include sexual intimacy. If this is the case, there is no real difference between the soul and spirit of a man or that of a woman even now. The only difference is the effect that the physical body temporally has on the soul and spirit while they are in this present body. If the body is temporary, which it is, and the soul and spirit are eternal, which they are, the care and development of the soul and spirit are the critical things in this life—not a provision for the body, even in marriage. It is most likely true that God trains the majority of us for eternity through the process of marriage, marriage intimacy, raising children, and dealing with making disciples of all people for the benefit of the soul and spirit. I also know that he uses the natural trials and tribulations and problems of this life to prepare us (soul and spirit) for eternity. I am sure that the physical body does give different perspectives, outlooks, and experiences to males and to females, but I would suggest that it is the same love, peace, joy, goodness, kindness, patience, self-control, gentleness, and longsuffering being developed in both male and female. If both males and females put as the first priority in their lives their relationship with Christ, they would find that it makes no difference whether they are male or female, but that either life would be totally satisfying, even with all the attendant problems of life.

~ A Man in Charge? ~

God has established an order of things. God has made the man the final authority in the family. Is this really a problem for women? Even in a fallen and sinful world? It is obvious that there is much turmoil between a husband and wife in this world. The cause of the turmoil is the sinfulness of the nature of the man and the woman. Each needs a heart transformation. Without Christ making that heart (mind, Romans 12:1-2) transformation, with the cooperation of those involved, turmoil (heartache, misunderstanding, hurt feelings, etc.,) will be the rule of the day. God has let our soul and spirit contend with a body that has a sinful nature in order to prepare our soul and spirit for heaven. It is my position that it does not make any difference which body one gets to contend with—the fight is exactly the same. There is no advantage of being in either body; to think that there is, is accepting, I think, a lie from the pit. I will admit that women face prejudice from males and find it harder to get the rightful respect and attention they deserve, with which the male does not specifically have to deal. However, being a male, I also know that men experience the same kind of prejudice from some males, organizations, clubs, etc. The trump card is that both male and female have a loving Heavenly Father who is a very present help. He can send you help or do any number of things for you—if you come to him for help! Try it!

God is more than sufficient to bless one in either body. An example that should be forever in our mind is that Christ, being equal to the Father, has forever submitted himself to the Will of the Father—to be totally obedient. The Father, in turn, has glorified Christ and given him all power and authority in heaven and on earth. (Matthew 28:18). God is able, and more than willing, to do the same for either a man or a woman, if he/she submits himself/herself to the Father of love and grace.

~ Conclusion ~

Being concerned with only the things of the physical world and denying the spiritual world, are the ultimate mistakes of mankind. To fail to put God first and above all else, which is common to mankind, is a serious mistake. It is too easy to address only the physical world and the false promises that the world makes to us concerning our well-being. Living to please God is not a natural thing for people to do. The just (righteous) will live by 'faith' and will please the invisible God of Heaven, who will forgive our sins, give us eternal life and joy, and glorify us in all eternity. Let those who have a heart to hear, hear what the Spirit would say. May God be able to bless each of us, because we seek to put him first place in our lives and to live a life of obedience to him, which is pleasing to him.

Larry Young became a Christian at the age of seventeen and has been a lifelong student of the Bible. His personal relationship with Christ, his Lord and Savior, and with his Heavenly Father and the indwelling Holy Spirit has resulted in his personal study of the Scriptures, where he has focused on theology in order to understand how "Christianity is supposed to work". Like all of us, Larry has personal and family struggles that have caused him to seek out "how things are to be understood" and "how to have the ability to live the 'truly' Christian life", even when life throws a few curves. This book is a result of that study, which he wishes to share with others.

In the true evangelistic spirit, Larry wants to convey his deep faith in Christ and his understanding of several questions that people have regarding their faith. In his book, he discusses the question of evil, the origin of humanity, the importance of attitude, baptism, judgments, and much more.

Larry is a 1961 graduate of St. Louis University, Parks College of Aeronautical Technology, with a Bachelor of Science Degree in Meteorology. Upon graduation, he was commissioned a Second Lieutenant in the United States Air Force and entered Air Force Pilot Training in April 1962. In July 1963, he attended the USAF Advance Pilot Training, becoming a helicopter pilot, which led to assignments in the Far East for a total of nine years, including three combat tours. The assignments included both 'fixed wing' and helicopter aircraft.

Over the years, Larry has participated in such organizations as Intervarsity Christian Fellowship, The Navigators, and The Kadena Overseas Christian Servicemen's Center and Air Force Chapel programs, the latter wherever he was assigned during his twenty years in the Air Force. Since his retirement from the Air Force in 1982, Larry has become a "Pulpit Supply" speaker for non-denominational pulpit supply, once filling the pulpit of a small non-denominational church for over two years.

A man of varied interests, Larry studied the Marshal Art of Judo, while in the Far East, becoming a Black belt in Judo and joining the Kodokan—the Japanese school of Judo in 1968.

Larry retired from the Air Force in 1982 at the rank of Lieutenant Colonel. He and his then wife, Rosalyn (Fincher) Young, and their two daughters and one son, retired to the small family farm located in Illinois, which Larry bought from his father in 1971. The family operated the farm, and Larry became a substitute school teacher, teaching mathematics and the sciences (biology, chemistry, and physics) for fifteen years. He still lives on the family farm.

Edwards Brothers, Inc.
Thorofare, NJ USA
August 10, 2011